# FUNNY
# How Things
# Work Out

## Chris R. Pownall

PNEUMA SPRINGS PUBLISHING UK

First Published in 2010 by:
Pneuma Springs Publishing

**Funny How Things Work Out**
**Copyright © 2010   Chris R. Pownall**
ISBN: 978-1-905809-97-4

Pneuma Springs Publishing
A Subsidiary of Pneuma Springs Ltd.
7 Groveherst Road, Dartford Kent, DA1 5JD.
E: admin@pneumasprings.co.uk
W: www.pneumasprings.co.uk

A catalogue record for this book is available from the British Library.

# FUNNY
# How Things
# Work Out

# Acknowledgements

I wish to extend my grateful thanks to the following individuals who have kindly assisted in some of the research for this book:-

- Mr Brian Thompson
- Mr Gordon Marlow
- Mr James Massey
- Mrs Margaret Massey – formerly Margaret Gibson
- Mr Jerry Simms
- Mr Jack Xiao
- Mrs Patricia Pownall

# FOREWORD

Following my retirement from work at the end of 2008 I decided to put together a record of some real life situations and stories that have amused me since my early childhood.

I have separated the book into five chapters, each capturing a stage of my life with stories and events appropriate to that time. I've done my best to string all these bits of information into a compilation that will keep interest levels high in anticipation of what might come next.

The first chapter covers my early school days and childhood in a Cheshire village. Chapter two is about my Engineering Apprenticeship at Wood Treatment Ltd, and things that happened around that time. My brief spell in the Merchant Navy as an Assistant Engineering Officer is covered fairly extensively in chapter three.

Chapter four is about my long service with James Walker, starting as a Trainee Sales Representative and finishing as an Industry Marketing Director. The final chapter is a collection of amusing stories that Pat and I recall after forty years of marriage.

My occupation has played an important role in my life and I consider myself fortunate that I have always enjoyed my work and the majority of those with whom I have been associated, during a total of fifty years continual employment.

They say life is what you make and I believe there is some truth in this statement, however, some are more fortunate than others and I put myself in this category.

If I could change just one aspect of modern living, it would be the poor attitude towards work of many individuals. If you are not happy with what you are doing, and if it is feasible, I believe you should try something different. You can't be laughing all the time but if you have a positive mental attitude plus a good sense of humour, then in my opinion, life can be more rewarding.

I have concealed some names where true identities might cause embarrassment and the last thing I want is to face any litigation following all the hard work searching my memory and the one finger typing that is now to a fine art.

I do hope you enjoy some of these tales and if by sharing things that have amused me, I can bring a smile or two to others, then I shall consider it, a good job, well done.

# 1

## Growing up in a Cheshire village

I was born the son of Robert and Lucy Pownall on the 29th December 1943. I have a sister named Cynthia who is eight years my senior.

My mother informed Cynthia that Dr Gillies had brought me in a black bag and I received a very tidy umbilical knot from nurse Nadine who attended the confinement.

I claim to have very good recall of my early years but there are sections where I struggle and I have a theory about this. Sadly my father died at fifty years of age, at which time I was aged nine and Cynthia was sixteen. I believe that young people block out such events, as they are too painful to bear, but having said this, I do have some memories of my father and they are all happy ones. I recall a situation when he and I were in the living room and there came a knock at the front door. Father answered and it was the local vicar doing his rounds. He was invited in and had just settled down in an easy chair when my mother Lucy who had been in the kitchen doing the weekly wash, opened the middle door and shouted "Hey up, the Parson's about". She hadn't seen him sat there but by our facial expressions she knew something was adrift. Can you imagine her embarrassment when she stepped into the living room and who should be sat there than the parson himself. Poor dear Lucy.

We lived in a council property in the village of Bosley which is located midway between Macclesfield and Leek on the Cheshire, Staffordshire border.

I attended St Mary's school Bosley from the age of five and I have good memories of fellow pupils and events, which took place. The head mistress was a very nice lady named Miss Roberts and there were a number of assistant teachers during my six years at the school, including

Miss Wigglesworth who was also a very pleasant individual. I clearly remember in 1953, Miss Roberts taking groups of pupils into her house, attached to the school, to see live coverage of the coronation of Queen Elizabeth II.

In those days only the wealthy had television and it was a year or two later before we joined those who could boast to having a set. Our first television was a nine-inch model, which stood on the floor like a large cabinet. It had a magnifier in front of the screen to make the picture larger and this worked well as long as you sat directly in front of the set. If you were positioned someway left or right of straight ahead, the picture became distorted and images were elongated which made people look like thin tall giants.

I guess life was very simple in those days, children were innocent in many respects and school life was pleasurable. We didn't do things like mathematics, they were called sums and we only had this subject in a morning as generally, the afternoons were taken up with things such as dancing, gardening in summer, and the occasional nature walk. If we had been extremely naughty then we might be punished with having to do some sums in the afternoon.

Before the end of each day, we had a short story read by Miss Roberts and this was always a nice way to wrap up proceedings for the day. Except on one occasion when someone made a hole in the seat of Miss Robert's high chair and inserted a pin with the point sticking upwards. When she sat down, she yelled out as the pin penetrated her rear end.

Sadly not all the pupils are still alive and I know that David Mitchell, front row far right, and John Greenhill, front row third from the left, both died as relatively young men. More recently, I understand that John Heath, middle row, second from the left, died. Miss Roberts passed away many years ago as would be expected.

Although school life was very gentle, when things did go wrong, there was a different way of dealing with disciplinary matters to what is allowed in this day and age.

Behind the pupils in the photograph is the boy's outdoor urinal and you can just see the entrance behind the girl with the white ribbon in her hair.

For a bit of amusement some of the big boys used to hold a competition as to who could pee the highest up the wall. On one occasion, we were lined up and spurting as high as possible when one chap out performed us all and cleared the top of the wall. Unfortunately for him, Miss Roberts was in the playground and she was caught in the firing line from the spray. She must have known who it was because without hesitation, she shot into the urinal and began smacking his legs furiously. That put paid to our bit of fun and I don't recall this particular sporting event, ever being repeated.

The picture below shows Miss Roberts's class in 1953 and that is me on the front row kneeling third from the right.

**Pupils at Bosley School 1950**

On another occasion someone wrote the big "F" word in a lad's new diary; he had proudly brought it to school to show to Miss Roberts. The word appeared on numerous pages and the lad reported the matter to Miss Roberts who immediately summoned all the big boys to the little classroom. She initially asked who was responsible for this and whilst we all knew the culprit, no one was going to tell. She kept repeating the word which she said she had never heard before and she was unaware of its meaning. Whether that was true or not, we shall never know, but needless to say we were all very embarrassed and pink cheeked.

The tall lad at the far right of the back row in the photograph is a farmer's son, Raymond Goodfellow and it was he that spoiled my illusion of Father Christmas. I remember going home from school on one occasion and saying to my mother that Raymond Goodfellow reckons Father Christmas doesn't exist. Sadly for me she confirmed that Raymond was right and I've hated him ever since!!!

The school dentist would visit about twice a year and this event put the fear of God into us all. The dentist and his nurse would occupy the small classroom and I can see the set up now. The drill was manually powered by a kind of pedal mechanism and the dentist would have the drill in one hand and whilst balancing on one leg, he would be pedaling away with the other. Such was my fear that I always managed to escape the school dentist and persuade my mother that we should stick to our family dentist in Macclesfield. He was no relation but his name was Harry Pownall and he had looked after our family's teeth for years. Fortunately for me I required very little dental treatment as a child until about the age of eleven, when I went for a check up and he said that I needed to have some first teeth extracted because they should have fallen out by this time. We returned for my next appointment and I recall sitting there in this fearsome red upholstered chair. All the instruments were laid out on a tray in front of me, which was enough to scare anyone to death. They used to say the dentist wouldn't pull your head off but in Harry Pownall's surgery; there was a human skull under a glass dome which beggars belief.

Harry gave me several injections and then approached me with the pliers. He removed four and that was enough for me, I leapt out of the chair, ran down the stairs and out into the street. I was closely followed by my mother, who gave me a clip round the ear. Still, I didn't go back in and the remaining first teeth must have come out on their own.

This story reminds me of a time when the school optician visited and I failed an eye test. We received a letter for me to attend an eye clinic in Macclesfield. My mother came along and we attended this special clinic in Pierce Street. We were sat in the waiting room when a tall gentleman in a long white coat came to the door and in a most unusual voice shouted "Christopher Pownall". Mother and I stood up and followed the man down a long corridor towards the examination room. The floor was shiny red and it had been snowing making the soles of my shoes wet. I slipped in a fashion whereby my feet shot out in front of me and I landed flat on my back, severely banging my head on the floor. I gathered myself up but by the time I was sat in the examination chair both my mother and I were in fits of laughter. I tried extremely hard to compose myself during the examination but it was near impossible and we were both delighted when it was finally over.

I was prescribed spectacles under the National Health and when they arrived I said, "I'm not wearing those as the kids at school will call them nashers". They had circular lenses, the type that John Lennon used to wear and they had spring type arms, which hurt behind my ears.

My Mother never knew, but I hardly ever wore those glasses and I was dreading going for another check up. Inevitably, the day came and off we went back to Pierce Street. The same man in the long white coat came out and as before, called out my name in the really peculiar voice. Immediately we started giggling and the embarrassment was awful. I sat in the chair and my eyes were examined again. To my shock and amazement, the optician said there was a vast improvement in my eyesight and I must continue to wear them like a good boy. I still didn't wear them or any other glasses until in later life, when I could get hold of more stylish ones.

In much later life at Cynthia's husband's funeral, I met a lady who I had not seen for some considerable years. I informed her that I could clearly recall her first day at Bosley School together with another girl from the village, named Muriel Johnson. I told her that Miss Roberts picked them both up and sat them side by side on her desk and said they looked like a couple of dumplings. Cynthia who was standing nearby and in clear ear shot said "you do talk a load of rubbish" to which the lady who's maiden name was Margaret Gibson said "no Cynthia, Chris is right, as I can recall the situation myself". That gave me some comfort as to the accuracy of my memory as I sometimes wonder just how factual many of these recollections really are.


Away from school, village life was also good and despite not having a father from the age of nine, my mother worked at the nearby mill and we didn't really go short of anything. Life was simple and we made our own amusement from what was around us. There was the River Dane where we could poach fish when local bailiff Jim Skellen was out delivering his post.

Michael Mitchell was one of my mates and we used to get up to all sorts of things. I remember us building a raft on the River Dane and looking back this was a very dangerous thing to do. The river was susceptible to instant flooding and several lives have been lost in such situations. However, we were not aware of danger in those days and the raft was built at the bottom of the weir at Higher Works. It comprised several barrels with timber boards strapped to the top.

Come the launch, Michael was at the front and I sat at the rear. We set off down stream, through the shallow rapids heading towards Lower Works. It was very precarious and as speed built up the raft became more and more unstable. As we approached the road bridge at Lower Works things were getting quite serious and I recall local poultry farmer Harry Yoxhall peering over the wall of the bridge, as he often did.

As we passed under the bridge the water becomes more turbulent due an adjoining contributory from the nearby mill.

Michael at the front was shouting and swearing, "sit still you bloody fool or you'll have us over" he yelled. Little did he realise, I was already in the brink and breast stroking my way to the riverbank. How he got off the damn thing I can't remember but I guess he must have realised my evacuation and abandoned ship.

On another occasion Michael and I were walking along the towpath of Bosley canal and moored at the locks was a huge barge containing things like sand and gravel, which Water Board workmen would have been using to conduct repairs. It was mid -winter and there was a thin layer of ice on the water. In our wisdom, we decided to take this barge for a trip up the canal. We found poles to punt the thing along and after untying the mooring ropes; we were ready to get onboard.

We decided the best way to get started was for him to stand at one end with me at the other. We both pushed with all our might and despite the thin ice, after considerable effort, the thing began to move away from the wharf. As momentum increased I made a leap and sat firmly on my end of the barge but when I looked at what Michael was up to, I realised that he was potentially in serious trouble. He had pushed too far and he was almost in a horizontal position, bridged over the water with his hands on the boat and his feet on the wharf.

Then it happened, the gap became too wide and in he went. Fortunately he was able to stand on the canal bottom with his shoulders out of the water. He was obviously seriously distressed by the extreme cold as he shouted, "don't sit there laughing you silly dick", "get me out of here quick".

I managed to drag him out on to the bank but what could we do then. We were miles away from his house and at least two miles from my home. It took great effort on his part to get back to our house at Penn Bridge where my mother laced him with hot drinks and provided dry clothes.

Before I move away from Michael, I recall a situation when we were a bit older and one particular evening, we had travelled to Macclesfield by bus to go to the pictures. Upon our arrival at Macclesfield bus station we purchased a packet of cigarettes from a vending machine. I believe the brand was called "Olivia" and we were very quick to light one up as by now we must have been at least 13 years old. It was big in those days to smoke and you felt really grown up with a ciggy hanging from the corner of your mouth. As we headed for the cinema, I spotted a policeman walking towards us on the same side of the road. I said to Michael "put your fag in your pocket until we pass this oncoming policeman". I did likewise but in my case the ciggy was concealed in the palm of my hand and not literally in my pocket.

As we passed by the policeman and he was far enough behind us, we resumed our smoking with great pleasure. We were approaching the cinema when I noticed sparks appearing around us and as we investigated, we were horrified to discover that Michael's brand new sports jacket was alight and one of the pockets had completely burnt away.

The evening was ruined and all Michael could do was to come up with something plausible to tell his parents. The best he could manage was to blame a hot radiator in the cinema, on which he had placed his jacket during the film.

As you can image, this did not wash and both he and I were in deep trouble.

There was a young lad in the village named Brian Thomson who would have been about four years younger than me. To say the least, he was a real character and always the center of fun. As a young chap he would stride through the village shouting such little ditties as "don't let your dingles dangle in the dirt". Brian's father Stewart was an Engineering Fitter at the nearby mill where I eventually became an employee and spent some of my apprenticeship working for Stewart.

Anyway, going back before then to when little Brian was I guess about six or seven years of age, one of the sons of the mill owner had a battery powered boat in which he was sailing up and down the feeder canal that supplied waterpower to the mill turbines.

Brian approached the scene and asked the boss's son if he could have a ride in his boat. "Oh buzz off" the boss's son replied. Brian repeated the question and received a similar response. "Stick your boat up your f***** a***" Brian replied. The following Monday morning Brian's father Stewart was summoned to the Director's office to explain his son Brian's behavior. I shall refer to Stewart in more detail in chapter two.

Back to Brian, he and I had an interest in guns and in particular gunpowder. I had discovered a recipe for gunpowder in an old encyclopedia and we assembled the ingredients including sulphur, saltpeter, charcoal and iron filings. One of our early missions with this gunpowder was to attempt to blow up a heap of council gravel that was positioned at the roadside for gritting during the coming winter. Despite many attempts, we were unable to get the damn stuff to ignite and following further research we found that to make the powder more volatile it required sintering and glazing. Sintering involves heat treatment after the ingredients have been thoroughly mixed together with water. My mother's fireside oven was selected for this process and the pieces of paste were placed on a tray in the oven and the door was shut tight. You are no doubt expecting to hear now of a disaster as the oven door blew off or worse still, the side of our house disappearing. No, this didn't happen but looking back, I break into a sweat when I think what might have happened.

The baked chunks of sintered powder were then tumbled in a makeshift rotating container, made from a used syrup tin and hey presto; we had ourselves something very volatile and dangerous.

We decided to make a cannon, which we could use to propel ball bearings by means of our specially made gunpowder. We managed to get our hands on a length of steel conduit, which came from the mill's electrical department. Ball bearings about a quarter of an inch diameter were readily found and these were a perfect fit in the conduit bore. We drilled a hole where the fuse would fit and we were about ready to try the thing out.

You would have thought we would have chosen some remote location for this experiment but no, not us, we decided to assemble the cannon on top of a stone wall which stood at the roadside directly opposite the mill offices. We lay the conduit flat on top of the wall facing towards the rear of the mill worker's parked cars. We placed heavy stones on top of the gun and then primed it with some of our special powder. Having had little success blowing up gravel dumps, we had resorted to using Jetex fuse, which was obtainable from model shops, and intended for the purpose of firing rocket propelled models. We had other ideas for its use and placed a length of fuse into the conduit and we were ready to go.

The fuse was lit and we placed our hands over our ears. It literally sounded like a cannon when it went off and there was a plume of smoke. We heard a metallic noise from the other side of the road and upon investigation; we were horrified to discover that the ball bearing projectile had made a hole in the boot of foreman Frank Marlow's Austin Somerset car. It was a highly polished vehicle in a fawn colour and it was Frank's pride and joy. Whether he ever found the hole I don't know but we kept a low profile and nothing was ever traced back to us.

I have good memories of James Massey, far left, back row in the school photograph. James was a few years older than me as the photo suggests. He was the only son of a highly respected farming family initially at Swallowdale Farm, Bosley and latterly at Cowley farm in Cowbrook Lane, Gawsworth.

Occasionally, Michael Mitchell, his elder brother David and I would visit Jim at Cowley Farm where we would fish for minnows in a nearby stream. Our fishing tackle was very basic and comprised a home made rod from a tank aerial with a simple fishing reel. We usually had the rod assembled and tied to the cross bar of our bicycle so that when we arrived at our destination, we were tackled up and ready to fish.

On one particular day whilst waiting at the farmhouse back door for Jim to appear, either Michael or David dared me to put a maggot on my line and drop it in the large rectangular tank used to collect rainwater from the roof of the house. Within this tank Jim had some fine rainbow trout, which were trophies of his fishing successes. I had no sooner lowered the juicy maggot into the tank when, whoops, there was a fish on the line. Jim was not best pleased as he appeared at the door to see me with one of his pet fish hanging in the air, attached to my fishing rod.

On another occasion, I recall visiting James alone and whilst taking a stroll around the farm, we came across a dead swan, which had obviously flown into some nearby pylon cables. I remember being amazed at the size of the dead bird both in wingspan and in overall length. We debated what if anything, we should do about this bird as somehow it didn't seem right to leave it to nature and we thought it was worthy of a decent burial.

We considered the easiest option to be a watery grave in the nearby Bosley canal and we assembled some wire from the farm with numerous heavy stones that we attached to the swan's enormous webbed feet. When the attachments were completed we hauled the dead bird to the waters edge and jointly threw it as far towards the middle of the canal as we could. In it went with a huge splash and very quickly disappeared out of sight. We were about to move on thinking what a good a kind deed we had completed when above the surface appeared just the head of the swan. It looked so funny and there was nothing we could do to change the situation. We just left it as it was but I occasionally wonder what people thought as they came across this peculiar sight, I can imagine someone strolling home from the pub on a moonlight night and the sight of the birds head appearing above the surface would be sufficient to give someone a dreadful fright.

Memories of Cowbrook lane bring back a recollection I have from my early teens. I was returning from a village dance in the early hours of one morning, pushing my pedal cycle up a steep hill on Cowbrook lane. It was a moonlight night and as I walked along there were steep grassy banks on each side of the lane with a small hedge growing on the top. I was shocked to the core by a large exhaling of breath that stopped me in my tracks. Some might think that in situations like this you run like hell but believe me, I was so scared that I was frozen to the spot. When I focused more closely, I could see that it was a sheep peering its head over the top of the hedge.

16

In the summertime some of the lads in the village used to earn extra pocket money by assisting local farmer George Goodwin with his haymaking. George lived alone and his farm was poorly maintained to say the least. The house was disgusting with the kitchen looking more like a pigsty.

George was happy for us drive the tractor or assist on the cart loading hay. George didn't use a baler in those days and once the dried grass had been forked into small heaps, it was lifted by means of a pickle fork, up onto the cart. Some of the hay was gathered by a huge fork attached to the front of the tractor. It's amazing that no one was ever hurt, working with poorly maintained machinery on fairly hilly terrain.

Typically we could toil all day in the hay field for the princely sum of half a crown which I suppose would be worth about five pounds in terms of today's monetary value.

I recall working late one summer evening and as we finished for the day several of us decided to visit the nearby canal for an evening dip in the nuddy. Jokingly, someone asked George if he was going to join us for a swim and to our amazement he said "yes". Off we went to our favorite spot on the Bosley canal, adjacent the first bridge, heading towards Congleton, where there was a nice concrete kerb from which it was safe to dive and the water was about six feet deep.

As we were getting our cloths off we heard a sound, which was something between a splash and a splodge. Goodness, it was George, he had dived in but not where we normally swam, rather he had plunged in on the other side of the bridge where there was a mud bank and very shallow water at the edge. He was stuck head first in the deep mud with his feet up in the air. We had to move swiftly in order to save him from a horrible death. We grabbed his legs and tugged until he was free. It took some time for him to recover from this frightening situation and afterwards we fell about in laughter at George's first late night dip in Bosley canal.


One of my childhood hobbies was messing about with simple radio sets. My very first success was to make a simple crystal set in a small matchbox. All you needed was a Germanium Diode and a coil of copper wire, which I wound myself. Seventy-six coils would tune to the BBC light programme. The only power came from a large aerial, which I slung from the bathroom window to the washing line pole at the bottom of the garden. To work effectively this basic radio set required a good earth and for this I connected up to the cold water supply.

Within the matchbox there were three nut and bolt connections to which were attached the aerial, earth and the head phones. Following a bit of fiddling with the homemade coil, the quality of reception was amazingly good. I can see myself now sitting on the toilet wearing my ex RAF headphones, wired up to this little matchbox.

We made a lot of our own amusement in those days and it was good for our general education.

Village life was simple but good and I have focused upon the happy and amusing times. Looking back, I sometimes wonder how we survived those more dangerous exploits but things were definitely different then. Children played out until late at night and parents had little concern about safety matters. Injuries did occur and I still have some scars to prove it. I remember playing football in the street and missing the ball and kicking the concrete kerb. The pain was excruciating and I struggled to walk home.

Mother and I were attending a wedding the following day and she claimed that I was putting on the agony in order escape the event. She bandaged my foot and off we went to Manchester. The pain was still there and I don't know how I managed to hobble about all day. We returned home in the evening and next morning I decided that something had to be done about this painful foot. I made my way to the main road and managed to thumb a lift into Macclesfield. I then had a long walk until I finally arrived at the Macclesfield Royal Infirmary. I reported to A & E and was asked to go to the X-ray dept, which was quite a walk in itself. Afterwards, I struggled all the way back to the waiting area until the X-ray results became available. When the film was held up to the light, you could clearly see that my right big toe was fractured and I was in a wheel chair before could say Jack Robinson!!

These are a selection of stories that I consider suitable for print but there are others that might cause offence and would certainly embarrass me. I trust I haven't given anyone the wrong impression and that my childhood credibility remains intact.

# 2

## Early stages of working life

Having failed my eleven plus, I attended secondary modern school in Congleton, Cheshire from where I finished full time education with no qualifications whatsoever.

At that time, my mother worked at the nearby mill in Bosley village and she made enquiries about possible employment for me. My father had worked there in the past and my brother-in-law; Cyril held a position as Charge Hand in the production area.

I left the secondary modern school at the Christmas holidays in 1958 just prior to my fifteenth birthday on the 29th December. An interview was arranged for me to meet with Mr. Gerald Thompstone, one of four joint owners and directors of this successful business. Mr. Gerald had responsibility for the engineering side of the business mainly focusing on new equipment and expansion of the manufacturing facilities. I had known Mr. Gerald as he regularly attended the local church and he often visited the children's Christmas party where he gave a cinematograph show to entertain the local kids.

On the morning of my interview I reported to the general office where I was shown to a waiting room. After standing there for a considerable time, I took a seat on one of the visitors' chairs and I had no sooner sat down when the door opened and in stepped a very large man who I had not seen before and had no idea who he was. "Don't you know that you should stand up when I enter the room" he said. "Sorry" I replied and explained that I was attending an interview with Mr. Gerald.

I'm Mr. Sydney," he said and I shall be conducting the interview in Mr. Gerald's absence.

This was a good start I thought, kicking off with a rollicking before being interviewed for a job.

"What would you like to do?" said Mr. Sydney, to which I expressed my interest in engineering.

After a few more questions he offered me an engineering apprenticeship, working in the maintenance department. My hours of work would be 8.00am to 6.00pm Monday to Friday and 8.00am to 12.00noon on Saturdays. He offered me day release from work to study mechanical engineering at a college of further education.

As I had no academic qualifications upon leaving full time education, I had to take a preliminary twelve-month course, which included subjects such as English, Science, Calculations and Practical Drawing. Classes for this preliminary course were held in the evenings, three days a week from 7.00pm to 9.00pm and this proved to be quite tough. They were very long days and of course there was lots of homework to be completed.

On the days of my evening studies, I worked the normal day at the mill and then travelled by bus to Macclesfield to attend college. I finally arrived home at approximately 10.00pm usually feeling very tired.

There were some real characters amongst my fellow students and a number of my recollections bring about a feeling of shame regarding the youth of that time.

We had a lecturer for technical drawing who was a bit weird and some guys used to take the 'Mickey' out of him. The lecture room for technical drawing was in the old building, which had a very high ceiling and steel tension bars supporting the roof beams. The lights were suspended from the ceiling on long wire cables with the bulb housed in a large circular enamel globe. During one lesson, there was a kind of tall step ladder that I guess the caretaker had used to change a light bulb. When the lecturer left the room, one lad climbed to the top of this ladder and began winding one of lights round and round, coiling the wire up like a spring. Someone keeping watch shouted the lecturer was returning, and down the ladder came the wind up merchant.

With the lecturer back in the classroom we were all in fits of laughter as we saw the light rotate first in one direction and then in the other. The lecturer was oblivious to what we were laughing at until disaster struck, the cable severed, and the light came crashing down. It was very silly because someone could easily have been killed.

The same guy who wound up the light almost wiped out an old lady outside the college.

It was wintertime and there had been heavy snow fall. At break time we would cross Sunderland Street to purchase a pie from Russell's butchers shop. Whilst standing outside the college enjoying our pies, the same guy who broke the light made a snowball and threw it way up into the air. I remember thinking that this must have been a record throw as it almost disappeared out of sight. It crossed the road and came down on top of an old lady's head and she was poll-axed to the ground. Again, not something I'm proud to be associated with, but it wasn't half funny at the time, though obviously not for the old dear.


I have a vivid memory of my first day at the mill and following a brief induction from Mr. King the foreman; I was put under the jurisdiction of Harold Yoxhall who was carrying out maintenance work on a piece of machinery known as a Plansifter. He explained that the work involved replacing the main shaft bearing. This was very interesting and there was considerable skill involved both in the removal of the worn bearing and in particular, when fitting the new one.

The bearing was located at the center of the machine in an awkward position and access was not easy. The new bearing had to be heated in a bath of oil to a precise temperature, which caused it to expand sufficiently so that it could be driven onto the drive shaft where it would shrink to provide a very tight fit.

When the bearing was heated to an exact temperature, it had to be assembled with the drive shaft very quickly before the temperature fell to a point where it would prove impossible to fit. During the preparation, Harold asked me to squat down in the space around the working area and he handed me a copper swage about 25mm diameter and 450mm long. This would be used to drive the heated bearing onto the section of shaft where it was required to sit. Harold explained that once he had located the bearing over the drive shaft, I should position the swage on top of the inner race where upon he would hit the top of the swage with a sledgehammer. It would require a number of blows at different locations to ensure that the bearing sat squarely in its final position.

I was quite up-tight about this procedure but he assured me that it was perfectly safe and I should not be concerned. I remember the distinctive smell of the hot oil plus the radiated heated from this large metallic component as Harold arrived at the scene struggling to lift the heavy bearing. He lowered it into position and I did as requested by locating the swage as I had been instructed.

On the very first strike of the sledgehammer, it skidded off the top of the swage and caught me a glancing blow to the head and from my very first day at work I returned home with a bump on my head, the size of a duck egg.

I spent the majority of my apprenticeship training working under a guy named Dennis Varley.

Dennis was a good engineer who had served in the Royal Navy and worked for the Gas Board on major installations. Later on, I worked with Stewart Thompson to whom I made reference in chapter one. Stewart was a very interesting character who was respected for his very quick turn around time. If something was needed to be done fast, then Stewart was the man. Whilst small in stature he was strong and enthusiastic about his work. For some reason he always wore Wellington boots, both in summer as well as winter.

Stewart was mainly employed on new plant installations except for those machines requiring immense patience and precision. For those jobs, another skilled fitter named John Bradley was generally given the main task. He had the patience of Job and because of his levels of accuracy we nicknamed him 'one thou Brad'.

I recall working through a Saturday and Sunday assisting 'one thou Brad' to replace a drive shaft and gearbox on a bucket elevator. The assembly took place with absolute precision and on Monday morning we still had some assembly and fitting work to complete before the main part of the mill could be started. A torque arm gearbox had to be secured to the final drive shaft by means of a tapered key. This key had to be size finished by using a hand held file and 'one thou Brad' was in his element performing such a task. He would file a little and then apply micrometer blue to highlight the high spots that had to be removed for a perfect fit.

On that Monday morning Mr. Donald, Works Director was on our case pushing for the maintenance work to be completed so that the wheels of production could begin turning. He was a man with little patience and having visited the scene several times he expressed his frustration at the loss of production and sent for Stewart Thompson. Stewart took one look at the state of the repair and disappeared to the engineer's stores, soon to appear carrying an assortment of fasteners and a lump hammer. He selected a suitable size coach bolt and hammered it into the keyway where 'one thou Brad's' perfect tapered key had been destined to fit.

Mr. Donald was very pleased as the mill started to turn but 'one thou Brad' was gutted as his wonderful keyway was now destroyed.

I could understand the rationale behind Stewart's action as the cost of downtime far outweighed the relatively small cost of another maintenance operation to fit a new shaft complete with precision keyway.

Stewart Thomson was not only a clever engineer but also a bit of an amateur entrepreneur. As well as his full-time employment at Wood Treatment, he was always pondering what to do next. Amongst some of his part-time pursuits was rearing pigs, tobacco sales to work colleagues and the production of fishing bait. When he and his family lived in Lower Works, he constructed a small plant in a disused cellar that produced ground bait, which he sold to local fishing tackle shops. I played a role in the design and building of this plant, which was mainly constructed, from scrap materials and surplus components from the mill.

Stale loaves of bread, which he purchased from nearby bakeries, were loaded into a hopper, from where they were heated to drive off the majority of their moisture. Then came a slicing machine that cut the bread into small pieces and following this, there was a grinding machine that provided the exact size of medium required for perfect ground bait.

Stewart would nip home at lunch break and top-up the feed hopper with stale loaves and take off the finished product, which was collected in sacks ready for delivery. The plant was fully automated and was a credit to his ingenuity. Although I never saw the finished equipment, I spent some time working on various components including the cutting blades.

This part-time business developed into a substantial enterprise and Stewart acquired a van for collecting stale bread as well as delivering sacks-full of the finished ground bait. Things were going very well and then one day, I clearly remember Stewart telling me that he had received a complaint about the quality of his bait. This was followed soon after by a series of complaints and Stewart was getting very concerned. Fishermen were complaining that when the ground bait was mixed with water and then thrown into the pond or stream, rather than disperse into a cloud formation; it would hit the water like a stone and immediately sink to the bottom.

Nothing had changed with the production process so obviously there was another reason behind the problem. Stewart contacted the bakeries from where he sourced his base product and coincidentally, the baking industry had introduced certain changes, which turned out to be the reason for the ground bait coagulating in the water. The changes involved switching from yeast to expand the dough to the use of carbon dioxide.

Stewart was unable to find a solution so that venture came to an abrupt end.

Not surprisingly, Stewart had lost one of his thumbs as a young man, apparently, when a homemade cannon exploded in his hand. This was a distinctive feature and it was interesting to observe how he had overcome this disability with his hands on engineering activities. He continually experimented either making firearms or other potentially dangerous bits of kit. I remember him saying to me that he wished to make a gas turbine and I advised him to be very careful. The project was still at the design stage and very early one Sunday morning there came a knock at our front door. It was Stewart and he was asking me to explain some mathematical formula, which he was struggling to understand. I was unable to assist him and again stressed the danger of what he was doing.

Typical of the man he went ahead and built a small working turbine and decided that the easiest way to conduct initial trials was to take it to the mill and connect it to the compressed air system. The story goes that as he turned on the compressed air, the turbine turned perfectly and slowly. He increased the air supply, which made the turbine rotate faster. He would have been very pleased with himself and no doubt, would have had some ingenious device in mind, for the turbine to power.

Unfortunately, as he continued to open the air supply valve, the turbine entered a resonance phase and to prevent it falling off the bench, he placed his good hand on top of the thing. Disaster occurred when the turbine disintegrated and part of his hand was severed. He was rushed to hospital but the only treatment, involved amputation just above his wrist.

This was a great pity and I'm certain that in this day and age, Stewart would have been a highflying design engineer.

Both he and I experimented with fermenting brews and it's a wonder we were never poisoned because we both made simple distillation plants. Mine was made from glass and I remember facing some difficult questions when I was purchasing the condenser tubes necessary for this illegal process. The reason I was not poisoned was because the finished spirit tasted vile. The base product was elderberry wine that I had fermented in five-gallon drums. Following three passes through the distilling apparatus it would ignite and burn with a light blue flame. My mother used to fear a knock at the door from the Customs and Excise Department but fortunately this didn't happen. Later on I realised how dangerous this activity had been and if the finished product had been of a different taste, then poisoning and even blindness were serious possibilities.

It was Stewart who gave me many of my ideas during those formative years. I recall seeing a farmer on the TV Tonight programme who had made a gas plant and he was running his Land Rover on home made methane gas.

That's a good project for me, I thought. I set about drawing the plans and assembling the necessary equipment. The base product was hen droppings that were contained in a chamber made from an old milk churn. Underneath the churn was a hot plate from a disused electric cooker and this was controlled by a thermostat immersed into the hen droppings. I constructed a 'gas-o-meter' from two oil drums and was able to purchase a compressor that had come out of a refrigeration plant. Other components included various valves and tubing, plus a pressure vessel and an electric motor to drive the compressor. I built the plant in our garden shed therefore I had to lay on a supply of electricity. Goodness knows what today's Health & Safety Executive would have to say about that project.

Once completed, the plant was fully automated and when the 'gas-o-meter' reached its maximum height, the compressor kicked in and pumped methane gas into the pressure container. I remember as a young apprentice rushing home at lunchtime to see how much methane had been produced that day.

This may all sound very grand but I never really got the thing to produce sufficient volumes of gas that could be put to effective use. Whilst it made methane that I could ignite in a Bunsen burner the quantities produced were disappointing. Doing more research, I discovered that I needed some seed bacteria to get the digestive process really moving. I tried this but to no avail and yet another Pownall project came to an end.

The mill as it is known, has a long history going back to the eighteenth century when it was a copper mill used to process copper sheet and wire.

The mill started a new chapter in the nineteenth century by becoming a corn mill and in the nineteen thirties it changed from corn to become a wood flower mill producing a product in high demand from the developing plastics industry.

There were two separate mills, the main one located at Higher Works focused upon the manufacture of wood flour and the other, situated half a mile down the road at Lower Works concentrated on the grinding of Mica which is used as a constituent in drilling mud, used as a lubricant in the Oil and Gas Exploration Industry.

Both mills had water-powered turbines fed from the River Dane by means of a canal and storage pool facility. The main line shaft at the wood flour mill could also be driven by a marine diesel engine and large electric motors. It provided good opportunity for apprentice engineers to gain a wide experience of many types of machinery.

In my early days working for Wood Treatment Ltd, the workers had no union representation and to secure an increase in your hourly rate, an appointment was required with Mr. Sydney. I recall one such situation when skilled fitter Harry Barlow met with Mr. Sydney in pursuit of a pay rise. Once Harry had made his case, Mr. Sydney referred to low inflation at the time and sited the very low cost of apples.

Harry made reference to his responsibilities towards his wife and four children, to which Mr. Sydney retorted, "In producing four children, you've certainly had the pleasure". Quick to respond Harry said, " If you saw my wife Mr. Sydney, you wouldn't say it was a pleasure". That was it, negotiation over; Harry came away with a couple of pennies increase, which was good money in those days.

Thinking about Harry Barlow I have an awful recollection whilst working with him on one of the water turbines. Harry was down the hole carrying out maintenance repairs and I was stationed at the top, required to lower tools down to Harry as he requested them. After some time stood there with nothing to occupy myself, like any young man, I became bored and to amuse myself, I began juggling with a King Dick ring spanner which probably weighed about 1kg. I started throwing the spanner into the air and following one revolution; I caught it in the same hand. I extended my juggling skills by increasing the number of turns in the air until my luck ran out and I dropped the spanner. It landed on the floor and made several dodgy bounces before disappearing down the hole where Harry was working. I recollect that fortunately he didn't receive a direct blow to his head but came up in a state of anger rubbing his shoulder.

There were several apprentices including a lad from Macclesfield named Trevor Byron. Trevor was not an academic but made up for this with his boundless energy and enthusiasm for the job.

The mill had a number of three wheel vehicles called Motor carts, which were mainly used for the transportation of wood chippings that arrived by rail. On occasion, the maintenance department would use one of these vehicles to transport heavy tools and materials. I shall never forget the time when Trevor and I had been working on a job together and with the aid of one of those Motor carts, we were returning with our toolboxes to the fitting shop.

The journey involved a short stretch down the main road and then a left turn into the entrance of the mill yard. Trevor was at the wheel driving the vehicle whilst I sat in the back together with two large toolboxes.

For those unfamiliar with the Motor cart design, they had three wheels including a single front driving wheel that resembled the rear wheel of a farm tractor. There were two smaller rear wheels about the size of car tyres. The vehicle was powered by a JAP diesel engine, integrally connected to the front drive wheel. The driver stood immediately behind the front wheel and steered by means of a vertically mounted steering wheel.

Surprisingly, considering that a Motor cart had only three wheels, they were remarkably stable but on that occasion, Trevor exceeded the stability boundaries and a near disaster occurred. As I have already stated, I was sitting in the rear section of the vehicle with my back towards one of the side panels for support. As we were travelling the short distance down the main road, Trevor did a silly thing and knocked the cart out of gear. It began accelerating at a considerable rate and as we approached the left hand bend into the mill yard, he lost control and in the back I was aware that we were tipping over. What must have happened in a second seemed to take ages as the horizon disappeared and I became airborne. This was a very lucky escape for both of us but in particular me, as fortunately I was thrown some distance clear of the upturned cart which would have cut me in two had I been caught by one of the wooden side panels. These were heavy vehicles and I would estimate this particular one weighed something like two tons.

There was a works canteen that was presided over by manageress Mabel. She would prepare and serve lunches as well as tea at the 10.00 am and 4.00 pm, 15 minute rest breaks. I recall someone allegedly witnessing Mabel dropping her knickers and putting them into a saucepan normally used to boil the lunchtime spuds. I don't know whether that was true or not. However, what I do know is that there followed a lot of cancellations for lunchtime meals

If you were one of Mabel's favorites you had cream off the top of the milk in your tea, which she managed by having numerous bottles on the go at any one time. As a favorite, I did very well but no doubt it was not good for my long-term cholesterol levels.

Having completed my apprenticeship and academic studies Mr. Gerald offered me a staff position working as a Draughtsman in the drawing office. This I accepted with great delight as it allowed me to extend my engineering experience, which would obviously serve me well in the years to come.

During the course of my seven years at Wood Treatment I have recollections of events that will stay forever. On my sixteenth birthday, I took delivery of a brand new motor scooter; a Lambretta LI 150 series one and this proved a gem in attracting the girls.

I remember my mother going away on holiday with Auntie Lilly from Macclesfield. Shortly before this she had purchased some new linoleum for the living room. They didn't have fitted carpet in those days and this high quality linoleum was Mother's pride and joy. Whilst she was on holiday with Auntie Lilly, I brought a young lady home on the back of the scooter and it was around this time when stiletto heels were the height of fashion. I remember as a student at technical college doing a calculation in applied mechanics, which proved that a stiletto heel created more pressure on the floor than an elephant's foot. This fact was proven to be correct on my mother's linoleum, for after the young lady had left there were clusters of indents around the settee where we had been canoodling. Needless to say the air was blue when my mother returned from her holiday. She had to purchase a small rug to hide the damage and repeatedly stated that she could not understand whatever we had been up to!!!

Before I had the scooter I used to travel to work by pedal cycle, which took no more than five minutes. As you approach Higher Works from where I lived at Penn Bridge, the road makes a steep decent down what is known as Chapel Bank. There is a slight right hand bend approximately half way down and a sharp left hand bend at the bottom, immediately before a level crossing over what used to be the Leek to Macclesfield railway before Lord Beaching wielded his closure axe.

I became very skilled at negotiating the last bend and at high speed; I would bounce across the level crossing usually on the last minute in order to get to work on time. As you descended Chapel Bank you could see railway signals in the distance indicating whether there was a train coming and if so, whether the wooden crossing gates would be closed. When approaching the final bend and level crossing at high speed it was essential to know that the way was clear as if you got it wrong, there was no chance of stopping in time.

One Saturday morning, I must have either misread the railway signal or not remembered to look but as I turned the bend it was horrible to see the large wooden gates shut in front of me. I immediately applied the brakes and the bike spun round as I crashed into the gates side on. To my embarrassment there were several people stood on the adjacent platform waiting for a train. I was completely winded by the impact and suffered some substantial bruising but survived to tell the tale.

I have very fond memories of the scooter and wish I had never parted with it as they are fetching a small fortune these days. I recall one not so good memory of one Saturday night when I had been to a dance the other side of Macclesfield. On my way home in the early hours of Sunday morning my trusted Lambretta died on me and no matter how I tried, I couldn't get the damn thing to start. I always had spare spark plugs in the toolbox but everything I tried failed. I was wondering what to do when a car pulled up and it was James Massey to whom I referred in the first chapter. I explained to Jim how I was fixed and he said "no problem", we'll put the scooter in the car. Whilst this might sound implausible in terms of today's cars, Jim was driving his father's Wolseley. It was a huge vehicle with running boards each side and a large drop down boot. We removed the windshield from the scooter and placed the rear seats of the car on the boot lid and this provided just about enough space to almost get the scooter into the back of the car. The only way to secure it was for me to stand on a running board outside, holding the scooter in the car by pulling on the rear carrier. It was hell but better than walking and I can remember passing the police station in Macclesfield praying that we would not be seen. We were very fortunate not to be spotted, but it was in the dead of night and the world went to sleep after midnight in those days.

I had borrowed a spanner from Jim when stripping off the windshield and I must confess that it was quite some time before I returned it. I bet a pound to a penny that he still has that same spanner which to me was worth its weight in gold. Thanks again Jim, your help that cold dark night was much appreciated.

My sister Cynthia together with husband Cyril resided at number 3 Higher Works in what was one of the mill houses. As a teenager I would occasionally visit them in the evening and we would watch television together. I was visiting one Friday night and during the course of the evening, Cyril offered me a piece of chocolate. It was in small pieces and I commented that I had not seen this type of chocolate before. He said it was new on the market and offered me several more pieces.

As I was leaving for home Cyril suggested that when I woke up in the morning, it would be advisable not to cough.

Thinking this was a strange comment; I paid no attention to it, and returned home to retire to my bed.

When I awoke on Saturday morning I was in agony with excruciating stomach pain. I slept in the nude in those days and as I reared my leg to vault out of bed, there was plume of excrement, which covered the white sheets on my bed. I recall covering the mess over in embarrassment and thinking what would my mother have to say.

As I was leaving for work I said, "By the way Mother, I have had an unfortunate accident and badly messed the bed. She thought I was kidding and laughed as I walked out the door.

It was a different story when I arrived home from work and she made me strip the bed and soak the sheets in an enamel bucket.

Cyril had fed me with Exlax laxative chocolate, which was very silly, but it obviously provided him with great amusement.

Both Cyril and Cynthia were part time bar tenders at the Harrington Arms in Bosley and when the incumbent manager Fred Austin retired, they applied for the job and were successful.

There are many stories but the one that is most prominent in my memory concerns my late Auntie Lillian and Uncle Walter. They lived in Burton upon Trent and they were regular visitors to the Harrington, usually for Sunday lunch. When the pub closed at 2.00pm, lunch would be served and afterwards, the family would sit in the lounge and enjoy a couple of cocktails. Both Aunt and Uncle very portly individuals and Auntie Lillian was quite a shy person.

This particular day, it had been a good after lunch session and there were more than the usual family party in attendance. It became opening time and customers began lining up at the bar. Auntie Lillian who was still sat in the lounge said she would retire to the upstairs accommodation until Uncle Walter was ready to return home. She sat on a low bench type seat and getting up onto her feet required considerable effort. Uncle Walter was stood at the bar ordering himself a pint of Worthington "E" whilst Auntie Lillian made several attempts rocking to and fro to get onto her feet. Then, with a final push she made it but unfortunately for her, as she left her seat, there was the loudest fart you have ever heard in your life. The place fell apart and everybody including customers were all in stitches. Poor Auntie Lillian made her way to the stairs door, wearing a very stern facial expression.

When she had gone, Uncle Walter sat down beside me and we were both still reeling from what had happened. I said how sorry I felt for her over this embarrassing event. Then Uncle Walter with a rye smile on his face said, "There's something you don't know, it wasn't she who farted but me". This was dreadful but I suppose you have to award him full marks for perfect timing. I bet the air was blue when she finally caught up with him.

A good friend of mine during those teenage years was Gordon Marlow who resided at 10 Higher Works, Bosley. He and I were drinking partners and I wish I had a pound for every bottle of Guinness that he and I drank during that period of time. We would visit the Blue Room in Leek, which was an early version of what would now be known as a discotheque. It was situated in an upstairs room at the Golden Lion Public House. On a Friday and Saturday night, the place was hectic to say the least. Geoff was the bar tender and disco player and he wasn't one to take any nonsense. At the least sign of trouble, he would turn off the music and sort out any disruptive elements. Geoff was a very heavy drinker and as the night drew on and he had downed at least a dozen bottles of Guinness, he would regularly turn down the music as a young lady was paying a visit to the ladies and yell out "don't piss on the seat", which always got a good laugh.

Towards the end of the evening, girls would be dancing on the tables and the atmosphere was terrific. You could hardly see for smoke as there was no ventilation and most people smoked cigarettes in those days. One record of the day that sticks in my mind is Chubby Checker singing "Let's Twist Again" and that would have been about 1961.

I have fond memories of my apprenticeship and time spent at Wood Treatment. It gave me the opportunity of a good grounding in mechanical engineering, which would serve me well in the future. Whilst my career was making progress at Wood Treatment, I had aspirations of grander things and became interested in the Merchant Navy. I applied to P & O and the Cunard line but at that time, they were not taking on Junior Engineering Officers. I saw an advert in the paper for a draughtsman at British Industrial Sands in Sandbach. I decided to apply and was successful in securing the position.

One evening in the Harrington Arms, a local businessman who frequented the pub, informed me that he did business with the Blue Funnel Line importing shoes from the Far East. He gave me contact details and I made a telephone call to the personnel office. "Give me your number and I'll call you back," they said. They asked me a lot of questions about my apprenticeship and academic qualifications and then invited me to an interview.

Before being engaged as an Engineering Officer you had to pass an oral examination by an Examiner of Engineers at the Board of Trade. This I did and passed with flying colours. Luck was on my side because one of the main questions involved how to fit a white metal sleeve bearing to a rotating piece of equipment. Towards the end of my apprenticeship at Wood Treatment I had done exactly that on a generator used for stand-by duties. I was familiar with the work involved and made a good impression.

*I was offered and accepted a position by Blue Funnel as an Assistant Seagoing Engineer.*

# 3

## The Blue Funnel Line

I joined the Merchant Navy in 1967 as a Junior Engineering Officer. I was with the Blue Funnel Line for less than a year as I soon realised that it was not the life for me. I suppose the experience broadened my engineering knowledge but the role of an Assistant Engineering Officer mainly involved watch keeping and ship maneuvers. Wherever possible, all maintenance work was carried out by shore-based engineers who operated to very strict planned maintenance schedules. In addition, we had on board, a full compliment of Chinese technicians who were very experienced and knew the engine room inside out. It was only on rare occasions that as officers, we actually got our hands dirty.

On my first day, I received an intensive induction programme and was accommodated in a nearby hotel that was owned by the Blue Funnel Line. I was one of a group of new recruits and for the first few days we were either attending lecturers or visiting the Company Medical Center where we were given quite a few vaccinations. I recall that following one vaccination for yellow fever, we were instructed not to take any alcohol for at least twenty-four hours. We took no notice of the instruction and spent the evening in the Pilot Public House downing a few pints of beer. That night we all slept in single beds in one large bedroom and in the night, one guy took a funny turn. He had developed a very high fever, no doubt from the yellow fever jab but I guess the beer had also been a contributory factor. He became delirious and was shouting obscenities and thrashing himself around the bed. The other guy and I were quite concerned of what might happen next and we pondered whether to call for some assistance. It was a very long night but fortunately by morning the disorientated guy improved.

One morning, the three of us had to attend a thorough medical examination that involved us stripping naked and then being examined by various doctors all in the same room. We were standing there in the buff when the door opened and in walked a very attractive young lady assisted on either side in her walking by two other ladies.

As one, the three of us being examined put both hands over our privates in total embarrassment. The young lady who worked in the admin offices had been taken ill and she had been brought to the medical center to see a doctor. It was a bit of a shock but afterwards; we did see the funny side of our reactions of modesty to her presence.

Following some initial training on various Blue Funnel ships in Vittoria Dock, I was assigned to a ship named the Pyrrhus, a 10,000-ton cargo vessel that had been built in 1949. We sailed around the UK discharging cargo, which had been transported from the Far East. This is known as coasting and involves both the distribution of an incoming cargo and the loading of goods for the next voyage. Newly recruited Officers generally serve on several ships whilst they are coasting as they undergo training in preparation for deep-sea trips.

Following a couple of weeks on the Purrhus, I joined another vessel named the Hector. She was also a 10,000-ton ship generally on the Australia run from where she had brought butter and fresh fruit to the UK.

Whilst I was serving on the Hector war had broken out in the Middle East between Egypt and Israel and Blue Funnel had two ships trapped in the Red Sea Bitter Lakes, following the closure of the Suez Canal by Egypt's President Nasser. This put strain on the Blue Funnel Line to maintain its scheduled services to Australia and the Far East with some eighty two vessels at that time.

At the end of World War Two, Blue Funnel had purchased a total of six Victory Ships from the government to increase its fleet numbers after major losses incurred during WW2.

Victory Ships had been built in the USA and were used during the war to transport essential supplies to the UK and Europe and their contribution to the war effort was invaluable. They were assembled from pre-fabricated sections and the total time for the complete build was little more than six weeks. They had all welded hulls and some of those that weren't torpedoed crossing the Atlantic Ocean suffered from hull fractures during heavy sea conditions and this caused some vessels to be lost.

The six Victory Ships acquired by the Blue Funnel Line were strengthened by longitudinal sections thus making them far more sea worthy.

One such Victory Ship was named "Talthybius" and she and another were brought back into service in 1967 to offset the loss of the two vessels the "Agapenor" and the "Menelaus" that were trapped in the Suez Canal.

A memo was circulated inviting all Engineering Officers to volunteer to serve on these vessels, which were to go on tramping duties, tidying up after the mainline ships assigned to scheduled services. Blue Funnel had an impeccable reputation for reliability and safety and you could guarantee that they would sail and return on time as near as was physically possible, taking into consideration possible adverse weather conditions. Due to this strict adherence to time schedules there was obviously cargo left behind by mainline ships that needed to be collected as part shipments. This activity was known as tramp steaming.

"Talthybius" had been built in 1944 by the Permanente Metals Corp (Shipyard no 1) at Richmond California with gross tonnage of 7,671, a length of 455 feet and a beam of 62 feet. She had a service speed of 15 knots and was powered by a three stage Westinghouse steam turbine.

She was a type VC-S-AP2 Victory Ship and was completed as the "Salina" Victory for the United States Maritime Commission in 1944. After the Second World War, she was acquired by the Dutch Blue Funnel line and renamed "Polydorus". In 1960 she was transferred to the British Blue Funnel line and again renamed, this time to "Talthybius". All Blue Funnel Ships were named after characters from Greek mythology.

I volunteered to sail on a Victory Ship and with a very good reference from the "Hector's" Chief Engineer, I was soon advised that I had been accepted as a Junior Engineer to sail deep-sea on the "Talthybius".

I joined her in Glasgow where she appeared a rusty old wreck. She had been laid up for several years in the Carrick Rhodes in Cornwall and time and the elements had taken their toll.

There were teams of fitters and engineers all working frantically to get this 'Old Girl' ship shape and prepared for a voyage to the Far East.

When I had told my officer colleagues on the "Hector" that I had been accepted to crew the "Talthybius" to the Far East, they fell about laughing and asked whether I had any knowledge of a typical Victory Ship.

**Talthybius**

When I saw "Talthybius" for the first time in Glasgow, I could appreciate why they had been amused at my action. This was nothing like a stylish Blue Funnel vessel with the typical naval architecture and sleek lines, renowned around the World for their elegance. It appeared more like a large floating barge with a straight foc'sle and a small funnel on top of the main accommodation.

Once on board and introduced to the Chief Engineer, I was shown to my cabin which was very basic to say the least. On board the "Hector", I had had a day room, which had nice furniture including a roll top desk and

37

windows providing lots of natural light. My accommodation on "Talthybius" was a single cabin containing a sleeping bed, a table and chair, and a sofa seat secured to the deck. There was a single porthole looking out on the starboard side of the ship.

Over the following few days things slowly began to look better and it's amazing what a difference a coat of paint can make. All the sanitary ware was replaced including a nice new washbasin in my cabin. New carpets were fitted and after the initial shock, I was beginning to feel quite at home on board this rather old lady.

Fellow members of the crew were a good bunch of guys although there was a great deal of practical joking. For a large company like Blue Funnel, there was a surprising lack of discipline over certain procedures and as a new comer you had to keep an eye over your shoulder as there was always someone wanting to take advantage of your naivety. I fell victim to this on several occasions when given false instructions by a Senior Officer. One guy asked me to pump the bilges whilst in port in Glasgow and afterwards, the water in the dock glistened like a rainbow from all the oil floating on the surface.

You hardly ever pump the bilges whilst in dock but if you have to, there is a centrifuge that separates out the oil from the water and this is used before anything is discharged into the dock.

On another occasion, I was asked to blow the boiler tubes, again whilst in dock. This is a process of blasting soot and scale off the boiler tubes and discharging it into the atmosphere via the ships funnel. By the time I had finished, the surrounding dock looked as if there had been a fall of snow except this snow was jet black in colour. I received serious rollickings following both these events but there was no alternative but to take it on the chin and learn from what had taken place.

Shortly before I joined the Company, one new recruit had a much worse experience in that he actually sank a ship whilst it was in Vittoria Dock, Birkenhead. He had been assigned to remove an inspection cover from a main engine condenser. He forgot to close a sea inlet valve and when the door came off, water flooded in and eventually, the ship sank to the bottom. Imagine the cost of emptying the dock, then re-floating the ship, and all the necessary drying out before it could re-enter normal service.

Briefly going back to the "Hector," I was fooled by fellow officers the night before sailing from Liverpool to Glasgow.

A ship during coasting would only have a Captain on board whilst it was at sea and this duty was normally carried out by captains who were fast approaching retirement age. During dinner on the "Hector", there was a lot of discussion between Senior Officers about the Captain coming on board for our forthcoming trip to Glasgow. It was Captain Davies this and Captain Davies that, all making him out to be a very nice chap.

After dinner it was my turn on watch and I had not been in the engine room very long when I received a telephone call from the bridge. When I answered it, the voice said "Captain Davies speaking." I probably said good evening or welcome aboard sir as you would in that situation. Captain Davies asked me to pump ballast water from one tank to another. This might seem a simple operation but a ships tank configuration is quite complex and you have to know precisely what you are doing. I was fairly confident in carrying out the transfer procedure but asked Captain Davies to repeat the references of the tanks from where and to, the ballast should be pumped.

I started the ballast pump and with a shiny valve key opened the valves, which would direct the flow of ballast seawater to where it was required. I had assumed that either Captain Davies or a Duty Officer on the bridge would contact me by phone when the required amount of ballast had been transferred.

After about half an hour it became apparent that the ship was taking a list due to the transfer of weight from the relocation of ballast.

In any ship's engine room there is an instrument called an inclinometer. It is attached to a bulkhead and shows the degrees of list from the horizontal. It's surprising our little deviation from the horizontal can be detected when walking about down below and I became aware that walking in one direction across the beam of the vessel was much easier than walking in the other. I looked at the inclinometer and it was showing a list of 5°C towards the quayside.

The emergency telephone rang and a red light flashed on the maneuvering platform. "What the bloody hell is going on down there," said a loud voice over the telephone. "I'm pumping ballast," I said as Captain Davies had instructed. "No such person on board" replied the First Mate who was very cross indeed. "Stop the pump immediately" he shouted "Were leaning on the f***n cranes up here" and you are going to have to pump the ballast back from where it came.

That was a typical practical joke, which is great fun providing you are not on the receiving end. I was responsible as a result of this activity for a new procedural instruction being put into place before ballast could be transferred. From that date onwards a signed permit had to be issued from the Senior Deck Officer before an Engineer was allowed to pump ballast.

The Officer in the next cabin to me onboard the "Hector" had a dreadful experience. He was required to start a diesel generator and switch it on to the electrical power supply. We were provided with clear but complex instructions on how this procedure should be carried out and this meant equalising voltage and balancing out current before engaging the main switch. He must have become confused and switched the generator when he shouldn't. He was thrown across the engine room floor and the contact breaker was badly damaged. I remember that I was in bed at the time, 5.00am in the morning and I was awakened by this very loud bang. Fortunately he wasn't seriously injured but he was in deep trouble as the damaged equipment had to be replaced before we could sail.

The "Talthybius" sailed from Glasgow down to Swansea where we took onboard steel plates bound for China.

Our next port of call was Birkenhead and upon arrival, I was given one-week home leave before the ship sailed for deep sea.

On the Sunday of my leave, my nephews were performing in something at the nearby Chapel and my Sister Cynthia asked if I would attend this event, wearing my smart new uniform. I resisted this and thought I would look very silly and embarrassed if any of my old mates were there. It did however cross my mind what we had been told before leaving for home. A Senior Officer had encouraged us to wear our uniforms whilst on leave, not all of the time but certainly for any special occasions. "Go on then" I said and reluctantly, we arrived at the Chapel. As we got out of the car, there was a heavy shower of rain and by the time we got inside my uniform jacket was rather damp. We sat in a row with my Brother in Law, Cyril to my left. There was a strong smell of varnish in the Chapel and it was obvious to me that all the pews had recently been treated. We sat there for about fifteen minutes and then the organ struck up and the service commenced. All bar me stood up but no matter how hard I tried, I couldn't move as my jacket was firmly stuck to the backrest behind. I called upon Cyril's assistance and he had to pull me forward by my shoulders and literally tear me off the seat. I was acutely embarrassed, even more so when the sermon was about perils of the sea. Gee was I relieved when that was all over.

Returning to the ship I discovered that I had mislaid my black uniform tie, but there was just enough time the following day to purchase another before we sailed for Singapore.

As the ship moved steadily away from the dockside several officers including myself were leaning on the safely rail observing all that was going on. I noticed a guy running down the quayside hell for leather with a small brown parcel in his hand. As he approached our ship, which was now several metres away from the quayside he shouted, "parcel for Pownall" and he spun it into the air and fortunately it landed safely on the deck. I knew immediately what it would be and sure enough it was my original uniform tie, which my mother had posted the previous day. Now I had two black ties as we embarked on our long journey.

Although "Talthybius" was capable of 15 knots, the Captain decided that we would cruise at a steady 11knots thereby saving fuel on our very long journey. There was also a safely aspect to this decision, as "Talthybius" was now approaching the end of her working life and there was much evidence of corrosion on the upper decks. On her previous voyage, she had lost part of her bow section in heavy weather and this had to be repaired before she could continue her trip.

With the Suez Canal closed, our route to Singapore was via the Cape of Good Hope and twenty-one days after our departure from England, we arrived in Durban, South Africa where we took onboard essential supplies. Our stay in Durban was only for a few hours and we then had another ten days at sea before we arrived in Singapore.

During the sail from Birkenhead, I had developed severe toothache and the Captain insisted that as soon as we arrived in Singapore, I should visit a dentist.

Literally as soon as we berthed, there was a limousine on the quayside ready to take me to the dentists. I recall that it was an American style Cadillac with Union Jack flags attached to each wing mirror. The driver took me to what was one of the very first skyscraper buildings to be built in Singapore and up on the top floor was the dentist's surgery. I sat in the waiting area where there was another merchant seaman waiting to have treatment. He was soon called and I could here something of what was taking place behind a screened off area on the other side of the very large room.

I could hear the clatter of instruments and grunts and groans and it all made me feel quite nervous. Then he appeared from behind the screens, with the nurse one side and the dentist on the other, they were supporting him walking as his legs appeared to be made of jelly. They sat him down and then invited me to go behind the screens.

"Before you begin", I said, "Whatever did you do to that gentleman?" "We extracted a tooth whilst he was under gas said the dentist." "You're not giving me gas" I retorted, so I had my tooth removed following an injection. It was quite painless and I sat there admiring the panoramic view of Singapore harbour.

Singapore seemed a very exiting place where a young man could have anything he desired.

My first proper trip ashore was with officer colleagues one of whom was married to a girl in Belfast and the other was engaged to be married. They were both looking for a good night but sex was not on the agenda.

Upon leaving the dock area we boarded a yellow cab where the driver said "what you want Johnnie, a girl, a blue movie or an exhibition". "Take us to a nice bar where we can have some drinks, a nice dinner and possibly see some girls", I said. The term in the Merchant Navy for going with girls is "bagging off" and my two mates were adamant that bagging off was not a consideration. The taxi took us quite a distance and we eventually arrived at what looked like a large mansion. "This looks like a fu-k-n knocking shop to me", said one of my colleagues. "Give over" I said, "let's go and investigate". The taxi driver offered to wait but I paid him off and said we would sort ourselves out later.

We entered this large detached property where we were met in the reception hall by a smartly dressed gentleman. "Good evening" he said, "can I get you guys a beer". The beers arrived and we sat at a table wondering what would happen next. The gentleman returned and asked if we were interested in seeing some nice girls. "Yes" I said, but my colleagues were uncomfortable about the situation. In tripped half a dozen or so gorgeous looking ladies all dressed in traditional costume and the gentleman said "see one that interests you". "How much" I asked. "One dollar for a short time and ten dollars for all night" he responded. Having studied the girls carefully, I decided to partake and pointed to the one with most appeal. My colleagues seemed disgusted and said they would wait for me outside.

The young lady escorted me to her room where I recall seeing many different bottles of perfume and other cosmetics. I turned around and she lay on the bed naked. "What do you require?" she said. "A short time for a dollar" I replied, which was equivalent to about two shillings and eight pence in those days.

The lady introduced herself as Yingtisha as I began to undress. I was ready for action when she said, "Aren't you taking your socks off?" this is a phrase that has stuck with me ever since.

Leaving out the detail, I was done and dusted in no time. The topic of conversation onboard ship was predominantly sex and we were all highly charged which didn't bode well for lengthy romps.

I paid my dues and returned to the reception area where again, I was met by the same gentleman. "Another beer" he said. "No thank you I replied", "my mates will be waiting for me outside". "No they won't," he said, "following a little encouragement by the girls they have both gone for a short time". How two faced can you get?

After nearly one week discharging most of our cargo from the UK, we put to sea heading for Borneo. We made two stops, one at the port of Labuan and the other at Jesselton.

In Labuan, we discharged a huge earth-moving machine that was unloaded onto a wooden jetty. With no tugs present this was a difficult manoeuvring exercise and required a great deal of seamanship so as not to demolish the jetty. I managed to get off the ship for a couple of hours and with a colleague; we walked down a clay path along the shore edge. To our surprise, we came across a guy stood next to a large refrigerator. As we approached, he opened the door and the contents of canned Guinness and Carlsberg lager was a most welcome sight. We stayed for a while and enjoyed several drinks before making our way back to the ship. I've often wondered where the electricity came from to power that fridge, as it was a long way from any obvious supply of electricity. Maybe it was powered by a portable generator or LPG.

Leaving Borneo, we headed for the Philippines where we made two stops; one at Cebu and the other was the capital city of Manila.

There wasn't a great deal to do in Cebu apart from negotiate with the natives over the price of large conch shells that had been decorated with a hand painted picture of our ship, complete with our name and Officer rank details. I still have mine although the years have taken their toll and some of the paint has disappeared.

Our arrival in Manila was interesting as there was a gun battle taking place on the quayside as our ship docked. Local police were having a shoot out with some bandits and the evening newspaper had a front-page photograph showing a dead bandit on the dockside with "Talthybius" in the background.

The Captain said we could go ashore but not alone and we must use only official taxis and be very careful how we conducted ourselves. Three of us left the ship and made our way to the dock entrance. At the barrier, we were approached by a guy in military uniform who asked each of us for one British Pound. In those days twenty pounds was the equivalent of one month's wages in the Philippines so he was asking for a lot of money. We refused to hand over any money and asked him to allow us to leave the dock area. He said he would shoot off our legs at the knees if we attempted to pass him without handing over some money. After some discussion, we decided to make our way back to the ship and then found another exit where we were allowed to pass without any problems.

Manila was a fascinating place and again a young man's paradise. The mini skirt was high fashion and the little Philippine beauties were a real treat for us sex mad sailors.

The Vietnam War was raging at the time and the Americans had built huge hotel facilities where the GI's were sent for service leave. Typical of the yanks they were destroying the economy with their extreme wealth and as a consequence, the bar girls had increased their previous rates.

I didn't manage to visit a suitable bar for a couple of days but our electrical Officer told me about a girl he had attended to and he said "Pownall, you won't believe your eyes". The following day, four of us went to this bar where sure enough, dancing with other girls was this little beauty and wearing the briefest of mini skirts.

It was a bit nostalgic as the bar was serving beer in pint jugs. Four pints were immediately ordered and then I beckoned over the guy in charge and expressed my interest in the girl with white mini skirt.

Things were soon arranged and I indicated to my mates that I was off to do business. She escorted me to a little room at the rear of the premises, where they had purpose built accommodation for lovemaking. Inside the room she whipped off all her clothes in no time and then dimmed the light. I remember switching the main bulb back on but she was having none of it and I had to be content viewing her stunning body by means of a five-watt bulb. It was all over too soon and I paid my dues and rejoined my mates. "I thought you were bagging off" one said." "I have", I replied. They fell about laughing as I had only been away from my table or few minutes and they were not even half way down their pints whilst I had done my stuff.

A few hours after leaving Manila, the city was struck by a major earthquake which would have caused us some serious problems had we still been there.


From the Philippines we headed for Shanghai in the peoples republic of China. Before entering territorial waters we were lectured by the Captain about dos and don'ts whilst visiting this country. It was the time of the Cultural Revolution and there was a lot of anti-British feeling particularly by the Red Guards. Our Captain assured us that we would be safe providing we abided by their rules and conducted ourselves like officers and gentlemen. He informed us that once alongside, we would not be allowed to leave the ship unless accompanied by official Chinese representatives. We could only visit two places, one being the seamen's mission and the other the seamen's shop, where souvenirs could be purchased. There was very strict control over currency and you had to retain receipts for all purchases made and then prior to leaving the country, all surplus cash had to be handed back.

We were instructed that unlike visiting any other port in the world, in communist China, you had to leave everything unlocked. Your possessions would be perfectly safe as the penalties for theft would either result in amputation or death. Our personal radios and cameras were confiscated by our Chief Steward who had them all locked away in a bond. Photography in China was strictly forbidden and we were in effect incommunicado until we left the country. Before arriving we were advised to inform our relatives that they would not hear from us for a period of at least five weeks.

As we entered the river Yangtze a pilot boat came alongside and several Red Guards boarded our ship where they would remain for the duration of our stay.

To enter the port of Shanghai, you leave the River Yangtze and enter a contributory called the Huangpu River. Having spent one week moored in the estuary, we received a signal that our ship could berth and begin working cargo. This was a relief to everyone as it was late summer in Shanghai and the weather was extremely hot with high humidity.

Once along side, the deck crew began unloading "Talthybius" of all the various bits of cargo that we had brought to this far off land. We were not made to feel welcome and for long periods of the day loud speakers on nearby buildings bellowed out anti-British propaganda such as "down with British imperialism". Whilst we were allowed some shore leave as I stated earlier, we could only visit the seamen's shop and the seamen's mission.

**A typical scene on the Huangpu River around the time of my visit**

The Red Guard positioned a century box at the foot of our gangway where an armed Chinese Officer checked the credentials of all boarding and leaving the ship. The procedure as far as we were concerned when requiring shore leave was to make an official request to our Deck Officer of your intention and the preferred time. A black limousine would arrive and you were transported free of charge both to and from your destination.

The seamen's shop had many splendid things for sale including camphor wood bedding chests but they were too bulky at least for storage in the very small accommodation on board "Talthybius".

The seamen's mission boasted the longest bar in the world and its main offering was locally brewed Shanghai beer.

I had visited both venues and like my fellow officers was ready to move on when having come off the night watch; the Chief Engineer summoned me to his cabin. "You are going ashore today" he said, we have received an invitation from the Chinese government for four crew members to go on a conducted tour of the city and surrounding area. I was very tired after being in the hot engine room all night but he would not take no for an answer so I made myself ready for the trip. My colleagues and I waited at the gangway at 9.00am for our hosts to arrive and we were somewhat surprised when a full size coach turned the corner and stopped by our ship. We were welcomed on board by several Chinese officials who presented each of us with two different Mao Tse-Tung badges and a copy of his famous red book.

We were invited to sit on the back row and off we went. A few minutes later, the coach pulled up alongside a Dutch vessel and about a dozen crewmembers got on board. They appeared to be carrying camera cases, which surprised us having had are photographic equipment put into bond. Following formal introductions the coach moved away and we were taken out into the countryside where we saw paddy fields and some cotton plantations. It was all very interesting and the Dutch guys were merrily taking lots of snaps. The coach then headed back towards the city and we were taken to an exhibition center where I had previously seen television coverage of US President Nixon visiting, during his recent trip to Shanghai.

It was all propaganda with boastful claims of technical advances under the Chairmanship of Mao Tse-Tung. There was an electron beam microscope, agricultural equipment, and their proudest exhibit was a compressed air cylinder, the type of which had been manufactured in the West for decades.

We were taken into a lecture hall where we were subjected to more boastful claims about the remarkable achievements of Mao Tse-Tung. Cigarettes were handed out and glasses of water that tasted unbelievably vile. Someone whispered, "don't drink the water because as soon as you did, they came round with a jug and filled your glass again. It was difficult trying to be respectful and polite whilst sat with a glass of water that resembled horse pee and a cigarette that could have been produced from camel dung.

Anyway, we survived the refreshments and back on board the coach, we set off to return to our respective ships. En-route we passed a spectacular stadium that had huge red flags all the way round its perimeter. The Dutch guys were learning out of the windows in order to get the best shots.

As we approached the dock area we could hear the sound of claxon horns and very quickly, our coach was forced to pull over by a number of armored trucks and armed soldiers were positioned to prevent anyone leaving. Our driver was physically removed and taken away in one of the vehicles. They put two soldiers on the coach but there was no communication as to what was going on. My colleagues and I sat across the rear seat smoking one cigarette after another. It was now becoming dusk and we were getting rather concerned that something was going very wrong. We could see the "Talthybius" blue with black stripe funnel illuminated in the night sky and one of my colleagues wanted us to make a run for it. I insisted that would only lead to serious trouble, because if we did manage to reach our ship, the century guard would not allow us to go on board and my worst fear was that the guards surrounding our coach would shoot us down as escaping prisoners.

After what seemed like ages, two black limousines arrived and a delegation of several men in long black coats came on board the coach. They made their way towards the back of the bus and in very good spoken English, one Chinese man said, "We understand that there are four English officers on board and would they identify themselves". They came to where we were sitting and asked whether we were in possession of any cameras to which we replied "no". They apologised for our detention and said we were free to return to our ship.

Once back on board, we briefed the Captain and said that we would not leave the ship again whilst we were stuck in Shanghai. It was only a few more days before we were ready to put to sea and as soon as we reached the Yangtze estuary and the pilot and Red Guards had boarded the pilot boat, we cheered with joy at the prospect of our freedom. You don't realise how fortunate we are living in a democracy and free society until you enter a regime such as communist China; it was good to leave it all behind.

Having escaped China, we were all looking forward to our next port of call, Moji in Japan. What a contrast and such a wonderful place to be; Moji was very welcoming and I needed to get ashore.

We were berthed at a mooring in the harbour and trips ashore were by means of a small ferryboat, which came every hour on the hour. It was my day off and I made an early start, not having to be back on board until my next watch, which was at 2.00am the following morning.

Having stepped ashore I wondered about this tiny seaport with nice shops and plenty of bars. I purchased some presents for my family including a musical Japanese doll in traditional costume and then decided that it was time for a beer. I entered this bar and whilst sat enjoying the first beer of the day, I was approached by a lady who asked if she could join me. Always the polite one, I said "yes" and she sat at my table. At first I didn't realise that she was a hostess girl but she started asking questions about what I intended to do for the remainder of the day and offered her services to show me around the city of Moji. She said we could have some lunch, then do some sight seeing and after dinner together, we could return to her apartment where we could make love. I told her that I would need to catch the 1.00am ferryboat back to the ship, as I was due on watch at 2.00am.

When asked about payment, she insisted that she would pay for everything during the day and I could then pay her in cash before I left. After buying my presents I had 9,000 yen in my pocket, which was the equivalent of £9 GBP. I just hoped that I would have enough money because we had several taxis and I thought the food and drinks might be quite expensive.

After dinner, we arrived at her apartment, which was very nicely furnished with the floor covered in a kind of rush matting. It was shoes off at the door and she took my coat and gave me a silk gown to wear. Before we could make love she insisted that we both took a bath. I should have already informed you that she was a rather mature lady; I guess she was probably about 40 years of age, very pretty and well kept. I had never made love to a lady of her age and I was greatly looking forward to the experience. She led me to the bathroom and removed all my cloths. The bath was a short one and it had a little wooden seat. I remember sitting there whilst she ran the water and began washing we down. I sat there and had to stop her from washing certain parts as our love making would be a very short-lived affair and it would probably be all over before I could get out of the bath. These are very clever ladies and know how to disarm a randy sailor, very often before he can get into bed.

With my bath finished she escorted me to the bedroom and wrapped me in the silk dressing gown. She lit me a cigarette and went off to bath herself.

I recall lying on the bed thinking this was going to be very quick, following the excitement of the bath. She returned to the bedroom also wearing a dressing gown and smelling absolutely gorgeous.

I did my bit which was all over in a few seconds and then she invited me to select some suitable music from her large collection of LP's. She had many Tom Jones records, which brought back memories from home. The green, green grass of home!

It was soon time to leave for the ferryboat and I nervously asked her how much I had to pay. To my astonishment she said everything came to 9,000 yen.

I remember the following day, informing our Chief Engineer about my experience when he fell about laughing, "don't you realise that she had looked in your wallet" he said. I must admit that it had not crossed my mind at the time.

Sailing from Japan we headed west and docked in Pusan on the South East coast of South Korea. This was only a brief stay and there was no shore leave available.

Leaving South Korea we sailed south for several days before arriving at Port Sweetenham which is the main seaport for the land locked capital of Malaysia, Kuala Lumpur. We berthed at a mooring buoy in the Klang River, which is a contributory to the Straits of Malacca. We found Port

Sweetenhan aptly named, as it was a steamy hot place with excessive humidity. The River was lined with mud banks where you could see very large crocodiles basking in the sun.

We had shore leave during our short stay although there was little to see or do. Several of us including our Electrical Officer and occupier of my adjacent cabin, made our way ashore by means of a small ferry boat, laid on purposely for our convenience. Upon landing ashore we were approached by a young boy, I guess he was no more that ten years of age and he offered to serve as our guide for the evening. He said that he knew all the interesting places that sailors would wish to frequent so we decided to give him a chance.

He escorted us through a very primitive village where people were residing in nothing more than mud huts. We eventually arrived at a nightclub, which we later discovered was mainly used by RAF officers who were stationed nearby.

The young lad explained to the doorman who we were and then, we were invited to enter the establishment, albeit, the doorman said the young lad would have to stay outside. One of us spoke out and explained that the lad was our officially appointed guide and if he was not allowed admittance, then we would take our business elsewhere. Following some discussion, we were allowed to take the young chap into the club and he sat at our table looking very thin and frail. The first thing he did was to stuff a bowl full of mixed nuts into his trouser pocket, which would probably be his best meal in some time.

At this stage the entertainment comprised a quartet of formally dressed gentlemen playing dance music of the time. Then appeared a number of very pretty ladies who sat around the room and we assumed that they were initially available as our dancing partners. We were approached by a guy who asked if we were interested in a dance with one on these ladies but if so, we would be required to pay a fee, which equated to about £2.50 in money of the day. This appeared to be extortion as for £2.50, we would be expecting much more by way of entertaining services.

We soon realised that we were well out of our depth in this establishment as it was obviously a retreat for well-heeled Royal Air Force Officers and beyond our financial means.

Not to be beaten, I invited our Electrical Officer to escort me onto the dance floor and we did one circuit of a quick step before making a hurried exit.

We then asked our boy escort if he could take us to a place where we might meet with some pretty girls and he set off in a direction and led us to what appeared to be nothing more than a large mud hut. The place was very interesting and the walls were covered in plaques naming ships whose crews had frequented this place, which was aptly named "The Jungle Bar". Sat down having drinks we were asked if we were interested in meeting some girls, to which we eagerly said "but of course". To our astonishment, an elderly lady was paraded in front of us before being positioned on a chair in front of our table. Some one said that she was at least sixty and not very pretty either. We were all very drunk by this time having had a skin full before leaving "Talthybius".

Our Electrical Officer asked the lady to let him see what he would be paying for and very crudely, he asked if he could have a blink of her Jack & Danny. Without hesitation she rolled up her long skirt to reveal her all which was not a pretty sight. I remember seeing lots of varicose veins in her legs, which was enough to turn off a randy merchant sailor forever.

We politely asked the man in charge if he could show us another girl possibly younger and believe it or not, there appeared a young girl who had probably not yet reached puberty. "That's enough," I remember saying, I am not into child sex and we marched out of the Jungle Bar in some state of disgust.

The following day we left this awful place and we were well pleased to be heading for Singapore where we knew what was available and we were certainly ready. Shortly after leaving the Merchant Navy, I saw an Alan Wicker programme which came from Port Sweetenham and sure enough he visited the officers club and reported on the extortionate fees charged by the girls including £2.50 per hour, just for dancing.

Back in Singapore, life was heaven with girls in abundance and everything a man could wish for. At this stage in a Blue Funnel voyage, Singapore was our last port of call before heading for home. Our coasting and tramping was over and although there would be stops along the way, we would officially be on deep see watches and en-route for our homeport of Liverpool.

During the voyage I had heard numerous references to gate five club in

Singapore and in my naivety I had thought this to be some kind of nightclub. We were each approached by the chief steward who instructed us to frequent gate five club before our ship embarked for home. Apparently, gate five club was a VD clinic where sailors could be checked out with all test results notified to them before they arrived home. Bearing in mind that nearly all the senior officers were married men; this seemed a very sensible procedure as the last thing they would wish the post man to deliver to their home was a report from the VD clinic irrespective of whether the result was positive or negative.

A fellow officer visited the clinic and upon his return, I joined him in his cabin for a report as to how he got on. I found him in a state of stress and discomfort following an examination and a swab test. "What happened?" I asked, and he explained that the examining doctor having taken a blood sample then asked him to drop his trousers. He like all of us had a sweat rash around his genitals having worked in excessive heat for months on end. The doctors took a sample of tissue from the area of the rash as well as a swab test from inside his John Thomas. He described horrendous pain as the swab was inserted and he likened the passing of urine to pissing red-hot needles. Naturally I was alarmed and frightened by this guy's experience and I knew that I too would suffer a similar torture having got a bad sweat rash in the nether region. I took only two milliseconds to decide that I would not visit gate five club and tell lies as it was company policy that all crew members be checked unless they claimed to be celibate.

Shortly before leaving Singapore several "Talthybius" Officers were invited to a party onboard another Blue Funnel vessel which had berthed in a nearby dock. I recall that as we boarded the ship in the evening, the walkway gantry was almost horizontal but several hours of heavy drinking later, when we were leaving the ship the gangway for disembarkation was at a steep angle as the high tide had lifted the ship several metres during our stay on board. As you stepped off the ship onto the steps, there was a horizontal safety rope at waist height, positioned around the top of the ladder. A fellow officer was in front of me as we left the ship and to say the least, he was very drunk. I saw him stumble as he stepped off and I closed my eyes as his legs went up in the air and he disappeared over the side. There followed a horrible thud as he landed on the dock below and I was convinced he would either be dead or at least, seriously injured. I braced myself as I peered over the edge and was very surprised to see him lay on his back with both eyes widely open. "Mind that fu--in top step" he shouted. We were very relieved that he was ok and it just goes to show that sometimes it pays to be drunk, and it might have been a different story had he been sober.

From Singapore we sailed across the Indian Ocean to the port of Colombo in what was Ceylon at that time. As we made our approach to Colombo I was called upon for standby duty. Standby is a state of readiness for the ship to be maneuvered both into and out of port. The engines are prepared so that they can be controlled both for speed and direction of the propeller shaft. Usually during standby, there are two engineers on the ships maneuvering platform to carry out changes in engine speed and direction as signaled and requested by deck officers located on the bridge. In this instance, I was asked to assist the second engineer on standby and he asked me to operate the ships telegraph and maintain the ship's log. Operating the telegraph needs some practice and is not as simple as it may appear. There are rules for normal requests signalled from the bridge as well as emergency calls when speed of action is paramount.

I had a bad time with the second engineer on the voyage and basically I hated his guts. Without going into details, he was very odd and his personal hygiene was appalling. When in the heat of the engine room, usually 123°F, the Second would sweat profusely and the smell of his perspiration made the rest of us feel sick. I had fallen out with this man on numerous occasions and we only spoke to each other as and when it was absolutely necessary.

I was not looking forward to standing behind him during standby, as I knew that as he wound the engine control valves, he would sweat excessively, stinking the place out.

In my experience of stand by duties up until that time, from the first engine change upon entering a port, there would typically be no more that twenty engine changes before the ship was stationary at its mooring.

As engine changes started on this entrance to Colombo, it was evident to me that something was different here as the request for engine changes were coming from the bridge thick and fast. Once you have actioned the telegraph, which advises the bridge that their request has been understood, the time of the request to the nearest second has to be entered into the ship's log. You are also required to enter any unusual events during standby that may be relevant to any later investigations. Both the Second and I were working our socks off trying to keep up with request on the telegraph for engine changes. The sea had a very heavy swell and we were aware that the ship was being tossed about and this made the task in hand even more difficult. Things got worse to a point where I was unable to keep up with the telegraph changes and enter the movements into the log. I remember the emergency telephone ringing and the red flashing light signalled from the bridge. I picked up the phone to be asked, "What in hell is going on down there". I had not realised it at the time but the Second had got into such a state that he was giving the incorrect movements requested from the bridge and effectively the ship was out of control. I was then aware of a very loud bang and entered in the ships log "bump" at the appropriate time.

We had crashed into the breakwater upon entry into the harbour but fortunately, neither the vessel nor anyone on-board was seriously harmed during the incident. Following the event, I was summoned to the Captain's office where-upon I was interrogated as to what had happened. I was completely in the clear but the Second was in some serious trouble. I recall thinking after the event that this could not have happened to a nicer bloke!!!


Our next port of call was Trincomalee, which has one of the world's biggest natural harbours. We were there to take on board tea and coconut fibre for transportation to England. Our arrival was at an unfortunate time as the tea growers and processors in Ceylon were on strike for better prices for their products and claiming exploitation by their Western customers. After about ten days, we were all getting very fidgety and bored as the ship was moored in the harbour and shore leave was not permitted. We were not even allowed to swim in the sea as there were reported to be many barracuda fish, which are very dangerous. In some state of desperation, some of us made a request to the Captain that we use the ship's motor lifeboat and take a trip ashore. After some persuasion, he finally agreed to our request but he laid down very strict ground rules. We were allowed to take the lifeboat several miles along the coast where we would find a lovely tropical beach with dense jungle up to the shoreline. The Captain made it abundantly clear that the Third

Deck Officer would be in complete control of the boat and be responsible for our safe return, which had to be before nightfall.

The motor lifeboat was built of wood in the traditional clinker construction and was powered by a small diesel engine. It was amazing how high above the water you felt when sat in the lifeboat waiting to be lowered by winches down into the sea. The Third Mate was dressed in his uniform and he took control of the tiller as we slowly moved away from the ship's side.

Before the trip we had been warned that in this area of Ceylon there lived a tribe of people whose way of life has remained primitive for centuries, this was thought to be probably due to the fact that they have all the food they required occurring naturally and they were very content living off the land and from fish out of the sea. We were advised to take with us some cigarettes and tablets of soap in case we encountered this tribe of people and then we would be armed with some useful and friendly gifts.

As we approached our designated beach we were more surprised than frightened to see an armada of canoes approaching our lifeboat. As they got nearer, we could see that they had brightly painted faces, which made them look very fearsome. The Third Mate stopped the lifeboat as the canoes came along side. We made haste and handed the natives a 200 box of cigarettes plus several tablets of toilet soap. Thankfully, they gave us agreeable smiles and proceeded on their merry way.

We beached the lifeboat and manage to secure it with a rope tied to a nearby tree and then we began exploring the surrounding landscape. We had a case of beer, which didn't last very long in the afternoon tropical heat; as we searched around for anything of interest. The only wild life visible was lots of white-faced monkeys, which made a dreadful screeching noise.

I happened to glance up at the sky and was shocked to see in the distance, what appeared to resemble a black curtain coming up over the horizon. We made an instant decision to head back to the ship and began our walk to the lifeboat. Upon arrival we were dismayed to see that the tide had retreated during our short stay and the lifeboat was almost out of the water. I'm uncertain of the weight of one of these old type lifeboats but it must have been in excess of one ton and as such it was impossible for us to push it back into the sea. I remember thinking that we were in deep trouble with bad weather or the end of the world fast approaching and no possible means of getting back to our ship.

In desperation after mauling ourselves trying to push the boat back into the water, we managed to find a couple of fallen tree branches, which we used to lever the damn thing into the sea. Once afloat, we sighed with relief as the Third Mate fired up the engine and we set off back to our ship. By this time the whole sky was very black and it was almost like total darkness. Rain began to fall unlike anything I have experienced before or since and it started to thunder and lighten, with the loudest claps of thunder that you can imagine.

I informed my colleagues that I had recently read an article in the reader's digest explaining how dangerous it is to be caught on the sea in an open boat, during a thunderstorm. Lightening strikes the highest object thus taking the least line of resistance. I lay on my back in the bottom of the boat whilst imparting this unnerving information to my colleagues and I can still picture the Third Mate sitting up at the rear with both hands on the tiller whilst doing his best to keep his head as low as possible. He like all of us must have been bricking himself.

It took some time but we managed to get back to "Talthybius" and whilst the sea was quite rough, by this time the worst of the thunderstorm had passed. As we pulled alongside our ship, they had considerable difficulty attaching the winch ropes due to a heavy swell. Finally we were very relieved to be back on board and you can imagine the rollicking we all received from the Old Man who had been ready to engage the services of the local sea rescue authority, as he had feared disaster. Needless to say, there were no more lifeboat excursions on this trip and I would imagine that our Captain would have taken a great deal of persuasion to grant permission for similar trips during the remainder of his career.

Leaving Ceylon we headed across the Indian Ocean bound for Durban, South Africa and following a few hours stay we made our way around the cape and headed north towards our last port of call before England which was Las Palmas in the Canary Islands.

The Canaries was a popular port of call for taking on-board boiler oil and this was our main reason for visiting.

As we approached Las Palmas, final touches were being made to the paintwork of the engine room. Blue Funnel had a policy of painting the entire engine room on the return trip following each deep-sea voyage. This activity was carried out entirely by the Chinese crew who took great pride in their work and once completed it was a most impressive sight. All bulkheads were painted cream with steam pipes red, fresh water pipes blue, sea water pipes green and oil pipelines brown. All this together with the brass components such as valve wheels being highly polished, all made the environment look extremely smart.

Now as I have mentioned, we were to take onboard boiler oil in Las Palmas and I together with a fellow officer were assigned to operate the various valves during the Bunkering procedure. I've not mentioned James Smith before but he had proven to be an interesting character during the course of the trip. He had suffered badly from seasickness and he had lost several stones in weight. I can recall one night out in Singapore before we embarked for home, he put on his best suit trousers and he could fold them twice before they fitted his considerably reduced waistline. James like me had made the decision that a life at sea was not for him and as we got nearer to home he became very excited at the prospect of leaving the ship for good. He became very silly and was clowning around as we began the complicated task of opening and closing valves, as the thick black oil was pumped onboard. The ship could take several thousand tons of oil and it was pumped at considerable volume to make the process as quick as possible.

We in the engine room had to open a valve at a time, which directed the oil to a particular tank in the bottom of the ship. There were sounding tubes emerging from each of these many tanks and as the oil flowed we had to drop a metal sounding tape, then quickly rewind it to measure the level of oil in the tank below. The skill was to gauge the rising level of oil accurately and as it approached the full mark another tank valve needed to be opened at the same time as the current one was being closed. This process meant that there was a continuous flow of oil and as one tank became full another one was accessed. If you got it wrong there was a risk of serious flooding and a risk of fire.

James was clowning around and pretending that the valve key in his hand was a microphone and he was singing merry songs at the top of his voice. As you might already have guessed, he cocked things up and we faced the embarrassment of a gusher of black thick oil spurting many feet up into the engine room and spoiling the surrounding paintwork which had taken weeks to perfect.

There was hell to play, with the Chief Engineer going bonkers. The Chinese crew worked day and night moping up the mess with sacks-full of cotton waste. They then had to repair the stained paintwork and it was just about completed when we finally arrived back into Liverpool. Before leaving Las Palmas, James and I made a pact that we would not visit the stern of the vessel other than in daylight hours. We were supposed to check the steering gear once a watch and this involved visiting the poop deck at the ship's stern. To view the steering gear, you had to descend through the Chinese living quarters and it is rumoured that a number of ships officers have mysteriously disappeared following confrontation with Chinese crewmembers. They had presumably been pushed overboard and following our problem with the oil, James and I thought that we might be at some risk as it was obvious that we were very unpopular despite all the overtime pay it provided.


Back in Liverpool, it was good to be back. It had been a wonderful experience but the life was not for me. Some guys were very relaxed and were more than content to read books and listen to music. I am not like that and need to have things to explore and toys to keep me interested. Life on board was mainly quite boring and time seemed endless. Maybe it would have been different had I been on a passenger liner but on the other hand this type of ship took me to many remote places that I would never have otherwise seen.

Blue Funnel was a very class distinctive company, which caused me some concern and annoyance. On the journey home I had been assisting one of the Chinese engine room attendants in learning English. He had purchased a "teach yourself English" book in Singapore and it gave me great pleasure and considerable amusement to assist him with the difficult pronunciations, flied lice, etc. The guy used to visit my cabin and whilst we did our English studies, I gave him a few beers. I was told that this should stop as officers should not associate with ordinary crewmembers and this made me very cross.

Also on route home I visited the Fourth Mates cabin, which was with all the other deck officers' quarters on the upper deck from where the engineers resided. My visit coincided with morning coffee and the Chinese steward came along at eleven o'clock with the usual coffee and biscuits. I made the comment that it was a pleasurable surprise to have some chocolate biscuits, as we were all tired of custard creams and "nice" biscuits. "What are you on about?" said the Fourth Mate, we always have chocolate biscuits. I was furious and protested strongly to the Chief Engineer. He was a good guy but he advised me to drop the matter as I was fighting a losing cause.

Overall, food on the ship was excellent but somewhat repetitive. Every night there was a formal dinner, which you had to attend in full dress uniform. There was a set meal for each day of the week and although I can't remember all of them, it was always fillet steak with a fried egg on top on Sundays and other dinners included, turkey chipolata, roast lamb and roast pork, Lunches were equally formal, when we were served excellent fish etc and Saturday was curry day.

When we were in port there was a deck pantry from where you could help yourself to a slice of meat from the fridge. Each day there was a full joint of beef or pork plus a selection of cheeses. No money was spared on food and all the deck pantry treats were replaced daily.

It was all very grand but we longed for such things as egg and chips or cottage pie.

Most of my memories of the Blue Funnel Line are happy ones and I'm glad that I made my decision to move on. Some of the guys on board that I had problems with were there under sufferance and wished they could escape. Salaries were good and individuals with wives and families to support lived up to their means and it wasn't easy to find work ashore and maintain the same standard of living. I feel that I was there just long enough to appreciate the experience and visit many far off places that I may never see again.

They say that you should never say never and in the next chapter I cover many more visits to Shanghai some forty years later and it was a great thrill when visiting Durban in 2004 that James Walker's Managing Director for South Africa, Aroll Patterson and his wife Migs, kindly took me to lunch at a fish restaurant in the same dock area where "Talthybius" had berthed for bunkers nearly forty years earlier.

**Engineer Officer Pownall pictured with mother Lucy 1967**

# 4

## Nearly forty years working for James Walker

Having tried the Merchant Navy and decided it was not for me, I took a job as a design draughtsman with F Bode & Sons Ltd, an engineering manufacturing company located in Leek, Staffordshire. I was introduced to the Company by Gordon Marlow, (previously referred to) a good friend of mine, and I was successfully appointed. This was interesting design engineering but it was a marked contrast to what I had been doing both at Wood Treatment Ltd and in the Merchant Navy. It was a case of standing at the same drawing board day in and day out and the job proved to be very repetitive. I pondered on what I might do; both from a job satisfaction point of view as well as advancing my engineering career.

I remember thinking about products used in the ships engine room that might be suitable for a technical sales activity. I considered pump and valve packings and sheet jointing materials and recalled that these items used on Blue Funnel ships were supplied by a company named James Walker & Co Ltd. I realised that similar products would be used in many other applications and industries, so I wrote to the Company head office located at Woking in Surrey, addressing my letter to the UK Sales Manager. I gave details of my career to date and expressed an interest in technical sales.

To my surprise, I received a response by return informing me that there was a vacancy at the James Walker depot, located in Hanley, Stoke-on-Trent. The reply came from Mr. R. M. Pullen, National Sales Manager and he suggested I contact the Stoke-on-Trent Area Manager, Mr. W. F. Seabridge.

I attended an interview with Mr. Seabridge and was offered a position as Trainee Technical Sales Representative.

Pat and I had recently married and money was tight. This change in my career would not be without risk and the job with James Walker had a strict probationary period. The salary was heavily commission based and I didn't know how successful I would be at selling until I had tried it. My research into James Walker showed them to be a long-standing company with a much wider product range than I had realised.

After considerable debate, Pat and I decided that I should give the job a go. The anticipated salary would be comparable with my earnings as a design draughtsman and there would be a company car provided.

At that time, Pat was working in the Cooperative food shop in Leek and before I received my confirmation job offer, she was visited at her place of work by Mr. Seabridge. He also informed me afterwards that he had inspected our terraced cottage in Duke Street, Leek that we were renting for £1.00 per week. He congratulated Pat on the cleanliness of the place and made particular reference to the curtains in the living room window and the polished front step. Being a man with high standards, he saw such things as character references. He always wore a smart business suit and very often, a dicky bow tie. His hair was cropped short and he looked the part of a professional businessman.

Whilst I was working my notice at Bodes Mr. Seabridge gave me a James Walker product catalogue together with a full set of technical leaflets and said that he expected me to be familiar with all the many products by the time I commenced work with James Walker.

My employment with James Walker began on 29th July 1969 when I turned up for work at the area depot, located at 114-116 Broad Street Hanley. I was welcomed by Mr. Seabridge who gave me a brief induction and then informed me that we were going to spend the day in Stafford.

I remember thinking that I had never been to Stafford before and wondered where we would be calling.

He drove to a major customer in Stafford and then presented me with a list of local customers. "I want you to take my car and call on some of these customers" he said "and then collect me from this location at 4.15pm".

Not much pressure as they say, this was my very first day in a totally new working environment, dropped into a city that I had never visited before and had to find some of the James Walkers' customers on the list that had been provided.

Obviously, there were no mobile phones or satellite navigation systems in those days, therefore I just had to drive around and find places the best I could. I soon sorted out the industrial areas and maybe by good luck I came across a large factory, famous for its compounds and adhesives. With no appointment and not even knowing whom to contact I parked the car in the visitor's car park and made my way to reception. I asked if it might be possible for me to see the Maintenance Engineer and I was pleasantly surprised when a gentleman in a white coat came into reception and called my name. We had a very good meeting and it was obvious that James Walker was a highly respected supplier of this company's sealing and gasket requirements.

I managed to find other customers in the area and returned to collect Mr. Seabridge for our return to the office in Hanley.

There was strict formality and it was always Mr. Seabridge when you addressed him, which was typical throughout James Walker at that time. I recall on my first visit to head office in Woking when some Senior Sales Representatives were addressing the chairman of the day as Sir.

In addition to Stafford, I was given parts of Stoke-on-Trent and Shropshire as my sales territory and I soon began to enjoy the job. It was interesting visiting many different companies and industries, and this was to broaden my mind as well as my engineering knowledge. Training within James Walker in those days was limited and you were expected to expand your knowledge by study and by asking questions.

The area was prosperous at that time, with a thriving pottery industry, and many others including, heavy electrical engineering, tyre production, pump & valve manufactures, breweries, gas & coke plants, etc. In addition to the wide spread of manufacturing companies, we did substantial business with power stations, water authorities, hospitals, etc. Telford Newtown began developing in the early seventies and several major manufacturers were attracted to the area. There was no shortage of business opportunities and we were able to grow our sales year on year.

I soon realised that the James Walker brand was extremely well known and respected throughout all types of industry and I was very pleased that I had made a good choice to venture into technical sales.

We all worked very hard and most days, I had to attend the office in Stoke at 8-30am, which meant leaving my home in Leek by no later than 7-30am. Following a briefing with Mr. Seabridge, I would then leave the office for a day's field sales activity and very often, it was 7-00pm in the evening before I arrived home. We also worked on a Saturday morning generally catching up on any outstanding paperwork and serving in the shop; they weren't called trade counters in those days. As well as carrying a wide range of high performance fluid sealing products, we sold many diverse items over the counter, including walking stick rubbers, fluted rubber matting, adhesives and lubricants.

Mr. Seabridge was an archetypal salesman whom customers respected highly. He had a reputation within the company, when there was something that could not be sold, send it to Wilf and he'll get shot of it. They were unaware, that if he couldn't flog it; it would be disposed of by other means.

Mr. Seabridge or Wilf as I shall call him from hereon was not only a boss but also a fatherly figure to me and very soon into my employment with James Walker; he encouraged me to buy my own house. He also suggested that I take out an endowment insurance policy for as much as I could afford and for as many years as possible.

I did take his advice on the property front and we moved into a brand new three bed- room house in Knypersley, Stoke-on-Trent. I remember Wilf coming to see the property and having given it the once over, him saying, "this will be worth at least £10,000 by the time of your retirement. Little did either of us know that I would sell it for £9,000 four years from then, having paid a purchase price of £3,000.


There was another sales representative at the Stoke Depot who was much older than me. Like Wilf he was always very well presented in a business suit and one morning he came into the office wearing a very smart sports jacket and matching trousers. Wilf took one look at him and said, "You are inappropriately dressed for business and if I let this go you will soon be coming to work in shorts".

Next morning when Wilf and I were in the upstairs office opening the post, I glanced through window and was flabbergasted to see the Senior Representative walking across Broad Street donning a pair of white shorts. As he entered the office there was total silence and Wilf without a flicker of emotion, left the room. It wasn't long after that; the same representative resigned from the Company.

Wilf was very strict about dress code, which was the standard expected throughout the Walker organisation and if you didn't like it, then you had a choice to make.

Whilst the Senior Representative was serving his notice to leave, I was asked to accompany him on visits to his major customers. At lunchtime he would eat his sandwiches in the car and then after loosening his tie, he would have forty winks for about half an hour. He swore by this and said it was beneficial in refreshing the body prior to a good afternoon's work.

At that time we had two very young children and Wilf used to ask why I always looked so knackered. "Because I get very little sleep," I replied.

Around this time I was paying my regular visit to Iron Bridge Power Station and as usual, I parked the car nearby and ate my sandwiches. Afterwards I remembered what the older representative had said about taking a midday nap and feeling very tired because of disturbed sleep, I slackened my tie and nodded off. Imagine the shock when I woke and it was half past five. Bloody hell I thought, I shall probably get the sack for this.

I debated what to do and took the decision to come clean and tell Wilf exactly what had happened. I remembered that during my interview Wilf had asked me what I would say to a customer if for some reason we were unable to provide a vital product and this had caused the customer to shut down his plant. My response to Wilf's question was to tell the truth and Wilf agreed that that was James Walker's absolute policy.

I visited the office next morning and with some trepidation, explained what had happened. He was very understanding and thanked me for telling the truth.

During my seven years working with Wilf there were many experiences that have stuck with me. Wilf was very much 'do as I say, and not as I do'. We sales guys were not allowed back into the office during the working day and if you really did need something, you drove past to see whether his car was parked in its usual spot outside the office in Broad Street. If all was clear, it was a quick dash to get what you required and then on your way.

Although there was a car park at the stores premises, Wilf would often park his car in Broad Street outside the office. On one occasion I needed something from the office and as I made my approach, I could see that his car was nowhere to be seen. I parked in the street outside the office and made my quick entrance. I had just reached to top of the staircase when there was an enormous bang and I feared the worst. I gingerly descended the stairs and my fears were born out when I could see that a passing vehicle had hit my car. It had been dragged onto the pavement and the off side body panel was completely damaged. As I was inspecting the wreckage, who should appear round the corner but Wilf. He parked his vehicle and then said to me "why the bloody hell did you leave your car there."

Betty Hood was in charge of the office and on occasion, she would lead everyone a merry dance. She used to arrive at the office late and then work on into the evening, sometimes until 9-00pm. I walked into the office one day to find two of the girls standing on their desks screaming something about mice. They pointed to a litterbin in which there were several mice that had obviously become trapped overnight. No more ado, I picked up the bin and took it to the ladies washroom where upon, I flushed them down the toilet. When I returned to the office that evening, I was summoned to Wilf's office where he informed me that all the office staff including Betty had reported me for cruelty.

Wilf was extremely patriotic and when the Queen was to visit Hanley, he sent me shopping to purchase some Union Jack flags. On the day of the visit, he closed the office and all the staff were lined up on the pavement, and instructed to wave their flags aloft when Her Majesty passed by.

James Walker had very strict rules regarding the use of company cars. There was a man based at head office named Reg Raply who was in charge of the transport department. You had to seek permission to use a roof rack and having gone through the process, I purchased a rack at the time we started camping. We had been on holiday in Scotland and decided to travel home overnight. That way, we thought our young children would sleep during the journey and the roads would be quiet. We loaded up the car including the boot and everything else was piled upon the new roof rack, including our nappy bucket that every family with very young children possessed. For those too young to remember nappy buckets, they were used to sterilize toweling nappies prior to

67

washing. The bucket was filled with water and a sterilising solution before the nappies were added. They remained there for a few hours before they were washed in the normal way.

I mounted the nappy bucket over two of the spars that ran across the rack and when all was secured, our journey commenced. Not long after our departure I detected a noise up on the roof but thought it was nothing to bother about. I stopped the car but all seemed well with the rack firmly in place, and with the sheet tied down, everything seemed ok.

It was a long way home but at last we arrived and I began unloading the rack only to discover what had caused that noise. The nappy bucket had slipped down between two spars and it had been sitting on the car roof. Having been at the seaside, I suspect there must have been some sand under the bucket and it had worn a circular area down to the shiny metal. I immediately thought about Reg Raply and I could see that I might be in serious trouble.

I sought some independent advice and purchased spray paint that did a pretty good job, and when the vehicle was returned to Head Office, it fortunately escaped Reg's critical eye.

Every couple of years, we made visits to Head Office for sales and product training. You would travel on Sunday and return home the following Friday afternoon. There was generally a group of ten Sales Representatives and the training programme was fairly intense.

As a break in midweek, we were treated to a visit to the Theatre Royal in nearby Windsor. Usually, it was a comedy and I always looked forward to the relaxation as well as the performance.

On one visit, we were informed by the National Sales Manager, Bob Pullen that the play billed for Wednesday was a melodrama and he asked if we all still wished to attend. There was a vote and the decision was made that the theatre visit would go ahead as usual.

Following dinner at a nearby restaurant we took our seats all in line, about three rows from the front stage.

Virginia McKenna was the main star and in the opening scene, she was thrashing around the stage, screaming her head off following a murder, there in front of our eyes.

Things on stage calmed down and there appeared a Chinese character in traditional costume. He strutted about the stage taking very short steps. He was obviously not a real Chinese man and his accent was particularly poor. Each time he appeared, I felt a strong urge to giggle but in the environment of a melodrama, decorum had to prevail.

I remember thinking if only he would go away thereby taking away the pressure to laugh. No such luck he kept coming on stage and the pressures became unbearable. Then it happened, I could sense that someone along our row was suffering just like me and there was a lot of nose blowing. I could feel vibrations coming along the row as individuals lost control. On my right sat the Assistant National Sales Manager and he nudged me and asked that I make them behave.

It was awful and each time this Chinese guy appeared the seat vibrations increased until we all lost control.

I felt very uncomfortable because you could see that the silly laughter was spreading and by now most of the first three rows were shaking in hysterics. I thought we were going to be thrown out of there and that those seasoned theatre goers who had paid good money to see a melodrama would be complaining about our very poor behavior. Then someone touched my shoulder and I thought oh dear, here we go. As I turned around it was a lady also in fits of laughter and she said, "please don't worry about the laughter, the play is useless and what she had observed in the row in front was proving to be more entertaining." That was a relief but I was still glad when it was time to leave as my sides were aching from the strain of trying to keep composure.

One of my last memories of Wilf relates to an evening when he and I were guests at the Stoke-on-Trent association of engineers to attend a lecture by professor Eric Laithwaite on linear motion. The event took place at the Kings Hall, Stoke and I can picture Professor Laithwaite standing on the stage behind a table covered with a whole array of apparatus. The Professor's invention involved the use of electrically generated magnetic force, which was harnessed to levitate and propel objects in linear motion. He showed us experiments to prove the concept and objects were flying off the table and shooting across the stage. I remember very clearly the Professor saying that people will one day travel on trains that run on a magnetic field and true to his words I have now had two rides on one of the early commercial versions of this type of train. I have travelled on the Shanghai Maglev train which runs from Longyang road station Pudong to the International Airport, Pudong, this being a distance of 30 kilometers. The journey takes approximately 7 minutes 20 seconds to complete with the train reaching a maximum speed of 431km/h (268mph). At max speed you almost feel as though you are flying. Good old Professor Laithwaite, it was great to see his invention put to commercial use.

Wilf was due to retire and not long after I was promoted to Assistant Area Manager at the Leicester depot.

Pat and I relocated to Syston, just North of the city and we had four very happy years in this vibrant area.

There was a very wide spread of industries throughout the area covered by Leicester depot that included Northamptonshire, Leicester, Nottingham and Derby.

I got to drive my first train whilst working at the Leicester depot. This came about when I was involved with the Chief Engineer of a Diesel Electric Locomotive builder. Following a design project on Locos destined for Iraq, he promised me that I could take one of the locos on a short test drive. I didn't really expect this to happen, but true to his word, he gave me a call and off I went to play with trains. The company had its own track, which connected to the main British Railway line. I sat in the driver's seat and cranked up the lever that controlled the speed. There were guys in white boiler suits carrying out final inspections as we drove along the test track. I remember sitting very high up in this shiny new heavy locomotive and it was a thrill that I shall never forget.


It was in 1982 that I was offered and accepted the Area Manager's job at the Sheffield depot. Once again the family had to relocate and we settled in the North Nott's town of Worksop.

Sheffield known as steel city because of the amount of locally based Iron & Steel manufacturing industry, was just right for me with my background and great interest in mechanical engineering. The scope for supplying James Walker packings and gaskets was enormous and in addition to the various steel plants, there were Mill Builders who had a global reputation for their quality of equipment used in the Iron & Steel manufacturing processes. I used to spend up to two days a week in the drawing office of one major Mill Builder where there were over one hundred design engineers, many of whom became good friends. Life was good in those days, I had an excellent team of supporting staff and sales were on the increase.

In the mid eighties business became more difficult with a global slowdown in manufacture and companies including James Walker had to look carefully at their cost base. James Walker had a network of regional depots that had been developed before the advent of the motorways and more advanced logistics throughout industry. Inevitably, the depot structure became unnecessary and a closure strategy took place, which eventually led to all depots closing with the UK Sales dept moving into a Super Sales Center located at Crewe in Cheshire.

Soon after this major restructure, the company decided to become more industry focused and I was given the role of UK Metallurgical Industry Manager.

I had a small team of Technical Sales personnel looking after the major Metallurgical Companies within the United Kingdom and in addition I looked after two global bearing manufacturers with head quarters based in the United States of America. I first began travelling overseas with James Walker in 1999 when I was asked to visit a major customer in the USA. From then on, I made approximately two trips a year to the USA travelling to Boston MA, Worcester MA, Chicago IL, Canton OH, Union SC, Torrington CN, Asheboro NC, Atlanta GE.

In October 2006 I was promoted to Industrial Marketing Director responsible for the global Metallurgical Industry. This new role was very exiting and challenging and involved a great deal of overseas travel. Until my retirement at the end of 2008, I visited the following countries: -

USA, South Africa, South Korea, India, Ukraine, Romania, Poland, China, Germany, France, Belgium, Luxemburg, Spain, Czech Republic and Ireland.

My main role involved Strategic Marketing and Business Development and for the two plus years as an IMD (Industry Marketing Director), I was very busy indeed, working or travelling most days of the week. Fortunately, my wife Pat was very understanding and my retirement was fast approaching when we could plan the rest of our time together.

Having given a broad overview of my long career with James Walker there are stories that I wish to share, hoping they bring a smile. Although I have always taken my work very seriously, I have a strong sense of humour and it is my belief that if you can enjoy what you are being paid to do and at the same time, have the occasional laugh, then your whole well being is greatly enhanced.

## Carefully check your hotel room

Whilst working as the Metallurgical Industry Manager, I was required to be at the Cockermouth factory for an early morning meeting. As usual in this situation, I travelled the night before and checked into a local hotel where Tim Smith, a fellow Manager would also be staying.

Tim would be involved in the following day's meeting and he and I had some preparation to complete during the course of that evening.

I arrived around 4-00pm and promptly checked in. As I was escorted to my room, I remember thinking how dark it was as we wandered along several corridors until arriving at my room. It was only a small room with a single bed but more than adequate for a one-night stay. I soon met up with Tim and we sat out in the evening Lake District air, finalising our work for the following day.

We had dinner in the main restaurant and afterwards, I informed Tim that I was feeling rather tired and wished to turn in early at approximately 10-30pm.

I made my way along the dimly lit corridors, turning several corners on what I believed to be the right track and finally arrived at what I assumed was my room. I was heavily laden with my laptop plus a number of large files on which I had been working earlier that evening. I remember struggling to find my door key whilst juggling with my arms full. I had several attempts to open the door and finally it swung open and I stepped inside. Having made two or three steps, I had a horrendous feeling that this was not my room and as my eyes accustomed to the dark, I could see a double bed in front of me and there were two people lying on the bed in a semi naked state. I stopped dead in my tracks and tried to back up to the door and make my escape hopefully unnoticed by the occupants. No such luck, as a rather stout middle-aged man sat up in his bed and said, "What the bloody hell is going on". "I'm terribly sorry", I said and continued my backwards retreat to the door. By this time the lady also in the bed sat up and screamed "oh God" as she rose up the bed head and then the wall. She was obviously very frightened and I guess I must have looked like a butcher stood there with my arms full of instruments, ready to carry out a ghastly deed.

At that moment, I made a dash for the door and shot along the corridor hoping that I could find what really was my room, then quickly get inside before I was in even more trouble. Whilst I moved very swiftly, I was not fast enough and the man from the bed appeared in front of me in a very confrontational manner. He stood there in his brief underpants; shaking with rage and asked me what the hell I was playing at. I tried my best to explain that it was a complete mistake and I was deeply sorry for any inconvenience caused. Eventually he calmed down and said something like "I'll sort this out in the morning".

As I got inside my room, I phoned Tim on my mobile and put him in the picture as to what had taken place. He said, "That could only have happened to you". I told him to forget our pre-arrangements for breakfast and that I should be up at the crack of dawn and out of there as fast as possible. I then sat on the side of the bed and broke into one of those hysterical bouts of laughter that only occur several times in a lifetime. I sat there and laughed until I cried. I recall thinking how much worse it might have been if there was a young couple up to any manner of things.

Naturally, I didn't sleep well that night and at 06-00am I was up, dressed and ready to go.

I very gingerly, made my way along the corridor, creeping past the room that I had entered by mistake, then down to reception ready to check out. There was no one to be seen but then the front door opened and a young lady stepped inside. "May I help you" she said, "Yes please" I replied, "I need to make an early start this morning. She removed her coat and sat at the reception desk where she began completing the paperwork. "Was everything alright for you sir" she said. "Yes" I replied but then I thought, this lot is not going away easily, so I might as well get my side of the story in first.

I explained to the young lady exactly what had taken place and she sat there in a state of disbelief. She said, "did that key open the other door", to which I assured her it had. She then disappeared and swiftly returned with the hotel manager who was completing his dress as he approached. I explained to him what had happened and he could not believe my story. "Look" I said, "I have told you the truth and now I am out of here before that very irate gentleman decides to come down to breakfast.

This was an awful experience but one that could have been much worse.


**Teamwork**

Jerry Simms was one of my Sales Representatives and he and I worked together for a number of years until he too was promoted to an Area Manager. Jerry, a very capable Technical Sales professional, has a wicked sense of humour that has caused me some embarrassment when we have been visiting customers together.

I recall a time when Jerry asked me to accompany him to visit the Technical Director of a company where there was a problem that needed sorting. As we travelled to this customer in Jerry's car, he said, "There is a very pretty receptionist where we are visiting and I'm certain you will like what you see".

Walking into the office, I immediately understood what he'd meant about the receptionist. We informed her that we had an appointment with the Technical Director who's first name was Richard. She stood up to reveal a very brief mini skirt and then disappeared into the factory.

Now this was going to be a very demanding technical meeting concerning hydraulics on a government trailer that was being built to transport nuclear weapons. As always in those situations, I would be tense and eager to get started. The factory door burst open and there she appeared again only to say in a loud voice", Dick will be up in a minute". I must admit that it struck me as being funny but for Jerry, he was creased up and out of control. Dick walked up the stairs to his office followed by Jerry with me bring up the rear. As I climbed the stairs, I could see Jerry's shoulders shaking and I had to start things off whist Jerry got himself together.


Jerry and I had several situations similar to that but he reminded me of another classic which occurred during Jerry's training period. As Jerry's Manager, it was my duty to provide ongoing training on Field Sales Techniques. We were out for the day when the subject matter was cold calling. I had intended visiting a Regional Railway Office to promote one of our specialist products used on permanent way systems. We entered the offices and a lady approached to ask whether she could help. I spontaneously entered into a sales pitch about our resilient rail pads and how they out perform those manufactured from re-cycled car tyres. As I made a slight pause, she intervened and said, "This is all very interesting but you do realise that these are the Head Offices of John Menzies the news agents". Jerry reckons it took at least half an hour to gain sufficient composure before entering the correct office.

I suppose the morale of this story is – that's how you do it Jerry, but make sure that you are in the right office!!

## You're spooking me

During my many travels to South Wales I would occasionally bump into someone I knew from my involvement with customers in Sheffield. There is one particular guy who I ran into on several occasions, more than you would put down to chance and during my first trip to South Africa I was working in the field visiting the major aluminium and steel manufacturing facilities when I spotted the same guy with a colleague of his. I was in a party of three and we were about to leave a particular plant when I said, "I know those two chaps over there". My colleagues looked aghast as I jumped out of the car and walked across to where these individuals were standing. "We shall have to stop meeting like this", I said. "What the hell are you doing here"? said one of the guys, "similar to you" I said. After all, we all work in the same industry therefore I consider it highly likely that our paths should cross from time to time. One of the men lived just around the corner from where I live in Worksop and he couldn't get over our chance meeting. The guy who I had bumped into in South Wales thought it spooky that I should keep running into him purely by chance.

That I thought would be the end of the story but strangely enough, a couple of weeks later, I had to attend an early morning meeting in South Wales and rather than travel the 220 miles the evening before, I decided to break my journey and stay at a small hotel in Ross-On-Wye. Ross is about 150 miles from Worksop so the next morning there is only 70 miles to go and then after the meeting it is reasonable to drive home.

I have stayed at the same hotel in Ross on many previous occasions; it is a very nice place with a good fish restaurant. I arrived early evening and having checked-in, I made my way to the bar for a refreshing pint of beer. I sat there on my own, it was the beginning of the week and I was the only customer in the place. After about an hour, I was making my mind up what to have for dinner, when I heard footsteps walking into the bar. I sat behind the door as you enter the bar and the person walking in didn't know I was there. The landlord served him to a pint and from the back of the guy's head, I knew it was, yes, the same chap I had seen a couple of weeks ago in South Africa. "Good evening" I shouted and he jumped; turned round and said; "now you really are spooking me."

He joined me at my table and we wondered about the odds of us meeting up again purely by chance. He explained that he had been travelling home that evening from South Wales with the intention of driving back to Sheffield. As he was feeling tired, he phoned his wife and informed her that he would stop off at Ross-On-Wye if he could get a hotel room for the night.

We had dinner together and whatever it was that kept bringing us together, went away, as I never clapped eyes on him again.

## Trips to the USA

I really enjoyed my travels to the USA, which usually involved visiting a major bearing manufacturer in Worcester, Massachusetts and another in Connecticut. This extended to other locations and to the James Walker manufacturing plant in Chicago. In the early days, I was always accompanied by David Steele, James Walker & Co Ltd Sales Director and sometimes by David Edwin-Scott, James Walker's Head of Technology.

We usually made two trips a year, flying out of Heathrow to Boston and then by limousine from Boston to Worcester. I made all the arrangements for the trips including hire vehicles as well as hotels.

In Worcester, we always stayed at the Crowne Plaza Hotel in Lincoln Square and dined in the evening at a nearby fish restaurant named "The Sole Proprietor". We would eat well on such delicacies as clam chowder; oysters and of course lobsters fresh in from Bangor, Main.

Following our business in Worcester we would travel by hire car to Connecticut where we enjoyed good business with another bearing manufacturer. The company was located in the quaint little town of Torrington and we stayed at a very special hotel called "The Yankee Peddler", located in the main street. This hotel is steeped in history and photographs dawning the interior walls show pictures of a by gone age when the hotel had a wrap around outer porch where old gentleman would while away the time on their rocking chairs.

When we visited Union in South Carolina, we flew down to Charlotte and then drove to Spartanburg in South Carolina, where we would stay overnight before completing our journey to Union, the following morning. The first time we visited Spartanburg we hadn't realised that South Carolina is a dry State and as such there was no bar in the hotel. Both David Steele and I both like our nightly tipple and no available booze was very bad news.

Not to be beaten, I made some enquiries and discovered that there was a small club within walking distance from our hotel where we could sign in using our hotel key as a reference. We decided to give it a whirl and it was OK, very noisy with hairy bikers and four televisions blasting away, but at least we got a couple of pints and a good steak.


## Cheap flights

Following numerous trips to the USA I made some enquiries and found that I could purchase return air tickets to Boston far less than travelling with British Airways.

I could purchase three return tickets for less than one economy ticket with BA and although David Steele was not keen he agreed to give it a go.

David Edwin-Scott was to travel with us on our next trip and I set about arranging the schedule. Everything had to work like clockwork when travelling on a business trip with David Steele and he was uneasy about the plan I had come up with. He once gave me a really hard time when we landed at Boston and there was no limousine waiting to take us to Worcester. It was a bitterly cold day and we had to wait whilst I phoned the company who then sent a van, which had mirrors on the roof and a video monitor. We assumed this vehicle was normally used for more seedy purposes and David was not at all impressed.

Regarding the trip I was now planning, we would travel with Aer

Lingus via Dublin and because both David's resided in Surrey, I booked them on a connecting flight to Dublin from nearby Heathrow and to save me having to travel to Heathrow, I booked my connecting flight from Manchester which is easily accessible by train from Worksop.

We had final discussions about the forthcoming trip on the evening before our departure and David Steele was still wary that things might go wrong.

Saturday morning came and I began my journey by train from Worksop to Manchester Airport, changing at Sheffield. I had allowed on hour spare in my journey time for checking in two hours prior to take-off.

On previous trips I would travel to Woking the night before and next morning, we would set off together by taxi and everything always worked perfectly well.

Back to this trip, I was on the train to Sheffield and no surprise; David telephoned to check that I was on my way. "Everything going to plan" I said, I changed trains at Sheffield and was now on my way to Manchester Airport. This particular train pulls into Manchester Piccadilly station and then reverses out and proceeds to the airport.

We had just cleared the outskirts of Piccadilly station when the train came to a standstill. There was an announcement that due to work on the track there would be a delay of 45 minutes. I began to get a little jittery now as my spare one-hour was slipping away fast. Sure enough, David phoned me again and I had to tell him that the train was at a standstill.

Approximately one hour later the train moved on and I gave a big sigh of relief. As I was approaching the airport, I received another call from David to say that the two of them had now checked in at Heathrow and as they were flying to Ireland, they were heading towards the bar for a pint of Guinness.

Having left the train I hurried along to the check-in desk and just as it was my turn, David phoned yet again but this time with bad news. He informed me that the main air traffic control computer for the UK had gone down and nothing was flying anywhere. I handed in my passport and asked the check-in clerk if what David had told me was correct. She asked me to keep quiet about it, as there would be an official announcement shortly.

David then came on the phone again and put me on to a representative from Aer Lingus who would advise me what to do. He asked me where I lived and then suggested that I go to the ticket office and re-book for the following day. He said that arrangements would change slightly on Sunday and whilst my flight from Manchester would go to Dublin, The two David's flight would now go from Heathrow to Shannon. My flight from Dublin would touch down in Shannon and we would all link up and travel together to Boston.

I made enquiries and there was no Aer Lingus ticket office at Manchester airport so I made my way to the main information desk. Having explained my situation, the attendant looked bemused and said that my flight to Dublin was a domestic flight and these had now resumed. She asked me to look on the screen and against my flight it showed go to gate. I hurried towards the gate, phoning David on my way to inform him that my flight was now on and we would be departing shortly. By this time, they were in a taxi on their way back home and David the boss was not at all pleased. "You make sure that there is a limousine waiting for us at Boston when we arrive tomorrow", he said

I was on my way to Dublin and I could now relax a little. On flights from Dublin to the USA, you actually clear US customs in Dublin so that when you land you are processed as if it is a domestic flight. I thought, that at least should please David.

I boarded the flight to Boston and we were ready to go when a very attractive stewardess approached me and asked if I would swap seats with someone so that he could sit next to his wife. I agreed and had just got settled again when she returned and asked if I would swap one more time. She smiled at me and said "boy I will look after you on this flight if you will accommodate my request. "Be steady," I said, I am a reputable married man and grandparent but I agreed to comply with her wishes.

We had not long taken off when there were signs that they were about to serve breakfast and I thought why are we not landing at Shannon which can't be far away from Dublin. I called the red head stewardess and asked why we were not landing at Shannon to which she replied, "You must be joking, this flight is direct to Boston". I then told her the story about what the Aer Lingus representative had said, that if I had changed my ticket for the following day, I would travel to Dublin and the two Davids would fly into Shannon. She said that was a load of nonsense and I began to panic wondering what kind of cock-up might occur when the two Davids resume their journey tomorrow. She told me not to worry and said, "they are big lads and they will no doubt look after themselves". Anyway I thought, there's nothing more that I can do now so I may as well sit back and enjoy the flight. As I was reflecting on a stressful morning, the same stewardess came to me and gave me four 50ml bottles of Gordon gin with similar amounts of tonic. She thanked me for agreeing to change seats twice and the drinks were for my cooperation.

We landed in Boston where my limousine was waiting and I arrived at the Crowne Plaza on schedule.

Prior to arrangements going awry, we had planned to practice a very important presentation on the Sunday afternoon in readiness for our meeting with the customer on Monday morning. With the two Davids now flying in on Sunday, they would be very tired after their journey and I was expecting David Steele to be more than a bit grumpy.

As I lay in my bed on Saturday night I thought I had better phone David and inform him about what the stewardess had said about the Dublin flight not touching down at Shannon. I tried his mobile several times but was unable to contact him. I then phoned my wife Pat and asked her to get in touch with him. She phoned me back to confirm that she had spoken to David and had expressed my concerns. "I bet he is concerned," said David who was obviously unhappy about how my travel arrangements had panned out so far.

The next day, I enjoyed myself playing golf with customer representatives and in the afternoon I contacted the airline to check if the flight was on time. To my horror, I was informed that the flight from Dublin was delayed by many hours and I estimated that the two Davids would not arrive at the Crowne Plaza much before ten o'clock Sunday evening.

I invited a customer contact who was also over from the UK and resident at the Crowne Plaza to join me for dinner and afterwards, we sat at the bar waiting for the two Davids to arrive. "For goodness sake don't laugh when they walk through the revolving door," I said and the clock kept ticking with no sign of them.

By this time, I was increasingly worried about them and wondered what might have gone wrong now. I was about to phone the airline again when they appeared looking very bedraggled. They had spent nine hours at Dublin airport and they were absolutely wrecked. I persuaded them to throw their cases into their rooms and join me at the bar so that they could unwind.

We laughed about it the following day and I explained to David Steele that I couldn't be blamed for air traffic control failures to which he said "no, but you do have a reputation for being associated with things going wrong".

We each made our presentations to the customer without a final practice and everything was fine.

Needless to say, we reverted back to British Airways for future trips to the USA and I was categorically told never to use Aer Lingus again. It was a pity for in my case, everything went to plan!!!

Whilst I have probably portrayed David Steele as a grumpy chap, he was excellent company to travel with and a true professional when it came to business. We had many good times together and I always appreciated his training and guidance as my career advanced.

## Keep on the right road

On one such trip to the USA it was just David Steele and I travelling together. We had done the Worcester bit and had finished up in Union South Carolina. It was part of my duty on these trips to do the driving and upon leaving Union we were to travel to Charlotte airport along Interstate number 49, a journey of some 90 miles. We had plenty of time for our journey and as usual if it had been a good trip David was singing Irish ditties and all was very pleasant. As we made our way through the sometimes barren countryside, the road layout seemed very different to the straight lines shown on the map. David was navigating and we kept heading in a general direction. The clock was ticking, there wasn't too much time to spare and we had not seen a road sign for several miles. Then one appeared, what a relief, a highway 45 sign. We sat back relaxing and once more the singing resumed as we journeyed on for several more miles. Then all of a sudden the "F" came from David's lips. " You silly bugger" he said, the 45 is the speed limit, and it's the Interstate 49 that we should be on". We pulled over and made some enquiries as to the error of our ways. We were about 15 miles adrift from where we should have been so we turned around and eventually got back on track.

## Up to our knees

On another trip to the USA, it was just David Edwin – Scott and I and as usual, we began in Massachusetts and finished up in South Carolina. It was late September and on the evening before we were due to fly to Charlotte from Boston I informed David that we would be walking out in tee-shirts the following day as we would only be 350 miles North of Florida. On the morning of our flight I was amazed to see on the weather forecast that there was a threat of a freak snowstorm over South Carolina. I didn't say anything to David and we made our way to the airport where our departing flight was on time. We sat separately on the flight and as the aircraft taxied out to the runway it stopped and the pilot made an announcement. He referred to a freak storm over South Carolina depositing 17 inches of snow and we sat there for one and a half hours. The guy sat next to me was a pilot and he said conditions in Charlotte would be dreadful as they rarely had snow and they were not equipped to keep the roads clear.

We landed in Charlotte and managed to collect our hire car for our 90 miles journey to Spartanburg. The roads were covered in snow and by now there was an ice storm making the roads absolutely treacherous.

This was David's first trip to South Carolina and I had told him all about PJ's club in Spartanburg but never dreamt we would encounter snow. It was a dreadful journey to Spartanburg and quite late when we arrived at our hotel.

"Come on Dave" I said, throw your case into your room and we'll set off for PJ's. Our only footwear was low shoes and as we trudged along the sidewalk, we were up to our knees in deep snow. Dave had a woolly hat on his head and I commented that he looked a bit like a robber. He was not amused and I had to work hard to keep him heading towards PJ's. Eventually we made it but we were very disappointed to find it closed and boarded up. There was nothing for it but to make our way back to the hotel. This was awful and once again my reputation took a big dive as I had promised a lovely autumn evening with pints of Sam Adams beer and corn fed steaks.

Back at the hotel, I ordered a taxi, which took us to a nearby restaurant where we managed to get something quick to eat before all the traffic came to a stand still.

The next morning, everywhere was frozen up with four inches of ice on the top of our car. I decided to abandon the trip to Union and suggested to Dave that we would head back to Charlotte.

Having struggled back to Charlotte, we quickly went to check-in. It was chaos with a queue stretching from the check-in desks back out of the airport building. With the freak weather, many airport personnel had failed to get into work so they were very short staffed. We queued for hours and having checked in, we then had to join another even longer queue to get through security. We spent the majority of that day standing in queues and we were both feeling very weary.

Eventually back in Boston we caught our flight to Heathrow but things were still to go wrong. We waited for ages at Heathrow for our luggage but alas it did not appear and standing in the long queue to report our mislaid luggage, David turned to me and said, "I shall never travel with you Pownall, ever again."

## Cancelled flights

A flight to Atlanta proved interesting and it all began at Gatwick when I went to check-in with Delta Airlines. As I entered the check-in area, I noticed a lack of people and within two hours to take off, you would expect to have found a lengthy queue. I handed in my passport and was immediately told that my flight to Atlanta had been cancelled. Oh bother, I thought, I have someone meeting me at the other end and early appointments the following day in Birmingham, Alabama. The check-in clerk said "not to worry sir" I have booked you on another flight but you will need to hurry as it is due to depart in 45 minutes. She checked-in my luggage and gave me my boarding pass and then pointed me in the right direction for a security check. As I was leaving, she said "by the way, the good news is that you going business class." I'm going back a few years and at that stage, I had not travelled business class before.

I hurried along to the gate and immediately boarded the plane, turning left, for the first time. Having taken my plush leather reclining seat, I was given a glass of champagne and everything in the garden seemed rosy. Another top up of champagne and things were even better.

Then there appeared a very attractive young lady wearing extremely well fitting trousers, who sat in the seat next to me. She was accompanied by two smart young gentlemen who sat in the two seats in front of us. She said to me "is that champagne you are drinking"? To which I replied, "I always drink champagne before take-off". She also started drinking champagne and I thought things couldn't really get much better than this.

Soon after take-off the steward came round taking orders for drinks and I asked for a gentlemen's measure of gin & tonic. He winked his eye and knew exactly what I meant. He then asked the lady next to me for her preferred drink and she too asked for a gentlemen's measure gin and tonic. The drinks duly arrived and they certainly were very good measures.

There was a lot of giggling going on between the lady next to me and the two guys in front of us and I asked if she would share the amusement with me. She explained that they were all three RAF (Royal Air force Officers) who had won the opportunity to visit Colorado on an outward-bound course. They had travelled down from the RAF station at Waddington and when they were checking-in, they were asked whether they would be prepared to fly to Atlanta instead of to Colorado. "Why should we do that they asked", and were told that if they switched flights to Atlanta they would each receive $400 each in cash and they would be upgraded to business class. She told me that she didn't even know where Atlanta is and she couldn't care less.

We finished our gin and tonics and she stood up to visit the toilet. "Order me another gentlemen's g & t whilst I'm away" she said. They really were strong measures and I could see they were having an effect upon her. We had lunch, which comprised fillet steak off a china plate, followed by desert and then the cheese board. We had white wine with the starter and red wine with the steak, finishing with vintage port and finally a large brandy. By the end of the meal, she was well and truly pie eyed and then I didn't hear from her for several hours. Eventually, she woke up complaining of severe headache. "What you need is another gentlemen's gin and tonic," I said but she was not amused and seemed rather livid with me for getting her drunk. "Don't blame me" I said, "You can take a horse to water but you can't make him drink!!!"

## Memphis, Tennessee

More recently, I was booked on a flight from Schiphol to Boston and this was cancelled at the last minute, causing major disruption to my planned business schedule in the USA. I had flown to Schiphol from Humberside and when checking into the executive lounge was informed of the cancellation. I then proceeded to the ticket desk to make alternative arrangements but with three hundred others it was chaos to say the least. I was travelling with my new boss and they were unable to find two seats on alternative flights. In desperation, I said just get me over the pond, anywhere in the USA and I'll settle for that. After much tapping at the computer, I was offered a business class flight to Memphis with two more connecting flights the following day.

Arriving in Memphis, I was provided with a hotel for what was to be just a few hours, but my luggage was travelling separate from me and was promised to arrive at my final destination. The only clothes I had were the ones I had left home in and by now, I was ready for a change. The thought's of going to work the following day without clean clothes and a smart business suit didn't sit comfortably.

I made enquiries at the hotel where I might purchase some new clothes and I was informed of a Wal-Mart store, located several blocks away. A cab was called and off I went to Wal-Mart, where I saw a lady attendant in a uniform and I asked her for some assistance. I explained my dilemma and asked if she could help me find two long sleeve white shirts, one pair of grey trousers, six pairs of socks, six pairs of underpants and one pair of smart black shoes. She hurried around the store and within a few minutes, there was only the shoes to purchase. One problem, the only black shoes available was Dr Scolls with soles about 25mm thick. If these are all you have, then I guess they will have to do. I paid the bill and boarded the cab, which had waited for me whilst I did my shopping. "Would you like me to take you to see Grace Lands?" said the cabby. "No thank you guv," I said, I'm very tired and just need to get to my bed.

The next thing I knew, it was 05.00am and my phone alarm was going off and my onward travels were about to begin. I took a white shirt from its packaging and put it on. I was shocked to discover that the sleeves came about four inches below the end of my fingers and there was that much fabric that it would have fitted a giant. Next came the trousers, which fitted my waist perfectly, but the gusset came almost down to my knees and by the time I had donned the shoes, I looked into the mirror and immediately thought of Charlie Cairoli, the clown.

I discovered afterwards that in the USA there are different lengths of sleeves unlike in the UK where collar size is the determining factor. I was so depressed that I took everything off apart from the new socks and pants and put on the cloths in which I had left home the previous day.

When I arrived at the customer the buyer said "Mr. Pownall, I never thought I would ever see you without a collar and tie". "No" I said, but I can assure you that I am wearing clean socks and knickers", to which he gave a cheeky grin.

### Problems checking-in

Shortly before my retirement, I was scheduled to take my appointed successor Francois Coeur on a trip to China and South Korea. We were booked on a flight to Shanghai from Schiphol departing at 6-20pm. Francois resides in Marseille so the arrangements were that our connecting flights would bring us together in time for the Jumbo flight to Shanghai.

A couple of weeks before the trip, I received an email from the travel agent informing me that my connecting flight to Schiphol from Humberside had been cancelled, but not to worry, as they had booked me on an earlier flight to Shanghai plus an earlier flight from Humberside. I informed Francois and suggested that we leave things as they were for now, and I would arrive in Shanghai approximately three hours before him but as we would be spending two weeks in each other's company plus the fact that they were night flights to Shanghai, it would be no big deal for us to travel separately from Schiphol to Shanghai.

On the Friday before our Saturday departure I told Francois not to inform our boss, as I knew he would try to change things and I better than most people know how readily things can go wrong. Francois did tell him that we were travelling separately and I received a telephone call saying that he had spoken to someone senior in KLM to try and get our flights changed so that we could travel to Shanghai together. I remember saying to my wife Pat that this could now end up as a mighty cock-up.

Saturday morning came and I arrived at Humberside to check-in. I was the first person at the check-in desk but very quickly the usual queue formed behind me.

I gave the check-in clerk my passport and she began typing in my details. "You are travelling to Shanghai on the 6.20pm flight" she said, and I then realised that my flight to Shanghai had in fact been changed and now I would be travelling with Francois after all. Out came my boarding passes but as the luggage labels appeared, the check-in clerk noticed that my luggage was booked onto the 3-30pm flight. She scratched her head and said she would have to make a phone call for clarification. She was on the phone for ages and I could sense impatience building behind me. Eventually, she came off the phone and said that she had now got things sorted. She tore up the boarding cards and luggage labels and started the check-in procedure again. By now things in the queue behind were really seething and I could here mumblings of people complaining. The second check-in seemed to take ages but eventually out came new boarding passes and luggage tags all showing me travelling to Shanghai on the 6-20pm from Schiphol.

I breathed a sigh of relief and as I was walking away from the desk she said, "you do realise that you are only booked on stand-by for the Shanghai flight. "Oh no", I said, that's no good; I am going on a business trip and need to have my seat confirmed.

There was no alternative but to start all over again. Once more, she went on the phone and a lady from the rear of the queue marched up to the desk and said "do you realise that we have all been waiting for 45 minutes and you have still not checked this guy in. "Sorry" said the check-in clerk, we seem to have some problems with Mr. Pownall's check-in today. "Yes" I thought and I know who has caused it.

Once again she tore up the labels and tags and began tapping away at the computer.

Finally out came the paperwork for the third time and when I was handed the boarding passes, I slipped away from the queue avoiding any eye contact. I swiftly made my way to the executive lounge where upon, I helped myself to a very large gin and tonic. I phoned Francois who by now was at Marseille airport awaiting his connecting flight. "Don't worry", he said, I'll try to get you changed onto the later flight when I arrive in Schiphol. "For goodness sake, no" I said, please leave things as they stand as if we are not careful neither of us will get to China today. The joys of travel!!!

## Working in China

My first business visit to China took place in 2004 when I was still employed as Metallurgical Industry Manager, and up until my retirement I made another five trips. My duties involved some training of technical sales personnel employed by James Walker's distributor in China, plus technical lecturers at the major Metallurgical Design Institutes. On each trip, I was accompanied by Jack Xiao who is the Sales Director for James Walker's distributor company.

Jack and I got on very well together, I rate his technical and sales ability highly and he is a very nice guy with a strong sense of humour. Together, we travelled extensively throughout this huge country, visiting all the regions where the Metallurgical Industries are located. Major cities visited included – Shanghai, Beijing, Dalian, Nanjing, Chendu, Hangzhou, Chongqing, Deyang, Harbin, Wuhan, Qiqihar & Xiangtan.

On my first trip to China in 2004, I was met at the airport by Jack and his immediate boss James and taken straight to my hotel in Pudong.

During the first trip, Jack and I took six domestic flights, which indicates the intensity of the work. The problem with the Metallurgical Industry in China is that it is spread over vast regions of this immense country. I immediately observed a different work ethic in China to the one now prevailing in the UK. In China they work extremely hard and seem privileged to do so. I know you can't generalise in these matters, but observing Jack closely over a period of several years and spending time visiting the Distributor's offices, I believed that I have a fair understanding regarding the Chinese attitude and commitment to hard work. I recall being in the Distributors' office one Friday evening and I asked the Managing Director, what time do they all finish on a Friday. "When all the work is completed" he said and from what I saw, this could be anything up to 9.00pm and beyond if the requirement was there.

The next time I visited China, I was met at the airport by Jack who this time, was driving his own car. He had recently passed his driving test and it was obvious from the beginning that he required a lot of experience.

Driving in a major Chinese city such as Shanghai is very demanding, with the volume of traffic plus the aggressive nature of taxis, I certainly would never contemplate taking the wheel myself.

On one of my early trips Jack decided to take me to Nanjing in his car and although this was frowned upon by James Walker's man in charge in China, Jack insisted and off we set. We were accompanied on the trip by a lady Sales Engineer who sat in the back seat.

As I have already stated, I respect Jack greatly and he is one of my favourite people. I don't wish to make fun of him, however, such was his driving in the early days, that I feel it my duty to share some of our experiences.

Jack is very fond of music and the CD player in his car is always switched on playing really nice music. However, he has favourites and they are repeated over and over again. I remember thinking that I shall be humming some of this stuff in my sleep if I have to listen for hours on end.

The other thing when Jack is driving is his mobile telephone, which rings relentlessly. He has those small earpieces that he has to fit each time the phone rings and all the time, the CD player keeps going at full strength. Whist all this is going on, he is at the wheel negotiating traffic situations that scare the pants off me.

Having made it to Nanjing in one piece, we then had to return to Shanghai and on the way back, I decided to sit in the back and allow the lady Sales Engineer to sit along side Jack in the front.

As we were approaching the suburbs of Shanghai, it began to go dark and I was observing that very few vehicles on the road had switched on their lights. Jack certainly hadn't and he was singing along to the music not showing a care in the world. I had noticed earlier, that the fuel gauge was on empty and several times I tried to draw the matter to Jack's attention.

It was nearly dark and I said to Jack "please put your lights on as we are in danger of being hurt", "ok" he said but still the lights didn't go on. We were overtaking large commercial vehicles some of which had no lights what so ever and others with something resembling a bicycle lamp.

Eventually, Jack put the lights on and then he noticed the fuel gauge. Panic set in and it was obvious that we were running on vapour only. We left the motorway at the next exit and luckily there was a filling station close by.

Over the course of subsequent trips, it was apparent that Jack's driving had improved and I became very relaxed with him at the wheel.

Whilst some would see my travels to China as a glamorous occupation, it was very hard work, not only with the busy schedules that Jack arranged for me, but from the physical demands of travel. I would take with me lots of samples and technical literature and whilst we maintained a base in Shanghai, I had to carry sufficient clothing for our extensive travels. The days were long and hard and most evenings would be spent entertaining Institute Professors and customers at traditional Chinese banquettes. Chinese food is very different from what you would find on the menu of a Chinese restaurant in our country and there would always be things on the table that would not be to my taste. Things like jellyfish, chicken blood, putrefied eggs, plus many others. Fish was always a good option but I rarely managed anything resembling a Dover Sole, typically, you would choose a fish from a tank and when it arrived at the table, it looked more like an Irish stew than fish.

I'm not being rude or critical of Chinese food as in many respects; their diet is far more varied and wholesome than ours. They have many types of vegetables and food plays a very important part in their lives.

Jack always looked after me regarding food and knowing my liking for prawns, they were always on the menu.

A typical Chinese banquette is served at a large circular table, seating up to twenty people. Dishes are served in sequence and there can be as many as twenty different delicacies over the course of a couple of hours. Eating would stop whilst they drank lots of tea and smoked like chimneys. I've seen Jack get through a full packet of cigarettes over a lengthy banquette.

I remember on one occasion, visiting a newly built aluminium plant close to Shanghai to give a professional opinion regarding a problem with overheating bearings. Following a mornings work, Jack and I were invited to lunch by the Plant Director and some of his colleagues. Jack said this type of entertainment is unusual in China and we should feel highly honoured.

Jack and I were accompanied by one of Jack's Technical Sales staff and we all made our way to a nearby restaurant.

This really was traditional Chinese cuisine and not for the squeamish.

There were live tortoises waiting to be slaughtered as well as large edible frogs, which were green in colour with large red eyes.

The Plant Director invited me to select five dishes after which, he said he would select a further five. I considered this to be a great honour and made my choices carefully. I remember roast duck being one choice as you can't go wrong with duck anywhere in China. The engineers' choices were far more traditional; the prize one being Chinese ancient style eggs.

We sat at the table and we began our meal. A bottle of the finest wine was chosen and we started to tuck in. I was to be tested as they sat me at the head of the table and I was asked to be the first to sample each dish when they arrived at the table. I was doing fine until it came to the eggs. They probably tasted fine, although I doubt it, as they looked revolting. Jack's assistant whispered in my ear that it is extremely bad manners to refuse special food in this way and that I should at least try a little. I am very tickled stomached, and if I had attempted just a morsel of this dish, I would have been very ill.

Things seemed to pass on and we finally finished our honorary meal to my great relief.


## Train journeys

Jack and I made several train journeys that were interesting to say the least. On one such journey, I had been suffering from traveller's diarrhea, which for me was par of the course on these trips. It is not serious and no way reflects poor hygiene; it is merely different bacteria to which we are not accustomed. However if like me you are affected by this disorder, then by the end of a two-week trip, you are feeling quite debilitated.

Before getting on to the train I had been particularly troubled with my stomach and had made several visits to the toilet before leaving my hotel. As the train travelled along, I could feel my stomach rumbling and the pain became unbearable. I gave Jack a nudge who by this time was fast asleep and I told him that I would need to visit the toilet. He screwed his face up and I didn't understand what he was trying to signal. Reluctantly, he led me to the toilet where on the lower deck there were two cubicles both with the engaged sign showing. I was in agony and to my relief one of the cubicles became vacant. When inside, I realised what Jack was trying to say as there was no toilet, just a hole in the floor. Fortunately, it was not a high-speed train so I lowered my trousers and assumed a squat position, holding very tightly to the support rail beside me. I soon realised that there was no toilet paper and just a tap on the opposite bulkhead to where I was squatting. I let go of the handrail and reached over to the tap filling my hand full of water. This was a very difficult balancing act and by the time I had moved my hand towards me, the water had spilt into my trousers. What a mess I was in and the only thing for it was to use my nice new handkerchief that fortunately I had in my pocket.

On another train journey, Jack and I were travelling to Harbin, which is located in the North East of China. As we took our seats in the first class compartment, I pondered what the steel bowls sat on each table were for.

The journey began and a lady came round selling refreshments. Jack and I had tea whilst the two other guys opposite purchased some snacks, which were sealed in clear plastic bags. They immediately opened up the bags to reveal large chicken type feet but I guess they were more likely from a turkey or similar type bird. They would snip off the claws and then I realised what the bowls were for. They were spittoons and once a claw had been snipped off it was spat into the bowl making a pinging noise as it landed. I have already explained about my tickled stomach and very soon I was feeling pretty grotty, as they munched away at these enormous feet they would pause to spit out bits of gristle and bone and the bowl was filling up fast. There then appeared another lady this time carrying an empty bucket, which she was filling up by emptying the spittoons as she passed along the corridor. My stomach was rotating and I said to Jack "Can you please try to purchase some beer." Off he went and quickly returned with four cans of beer called Hapi Beer produced by a very famous brewery in Harbin. Most beers in China are very weak, typically 2% ABV but this Hapi beer was a good 5% and I was soon feeling some relief. Drinking the beer, I disciplined myself to look through the window and thereby avoid seeing the spitting that was going on all around me.

Jack left his seat again and returned with still more Hapi beer and by the end of our journey, we were both feeling very happy indeed.

## Harbin fish

On another visit to Harbin, Jack insisted on taking me to a famous fish restaurant situated on the banks of the Songhua River. We had arrived late and I was very tired after much travelling. Jack is a very persistent person and he would not be dissuaded from taking me to this fish restaurant. We took a taxi, which soon left the good roads and took to really rough terrain. It was a bumpy ride and after about twenty minutes we arrived at our destination, where there were four adjacent restaurants on the riverbank. I should have said earlier that about six months prior to this trip, there had been a serious chemical leak into the Songhua River following an explosion at a nearby chemical works. The disaster was referred to on the BBC news but there was very little detail about the number of casualties. I had tried earlier to put Jack off from eating fish out of the river but as usual his mind was made up and that was that.

The Songhua River flows north from China into Russia and it looks very muddy as it passes through the center of Harbin.

As we got out of our taxi, we were descended upon by staff from each of the four restaurants. Jack decided to look inside all four before making up his mind.

They all looked very similar to me, being quite primitive and dimly lit. Each restaurant had a make shift pond at the rear which had been created by a plastic sheet placed in a prepared hole in the ground. In these ponds were large river carp and the restaurant staff took nets hauling different fish out of the water thereby tempting our appetites.

Jack made a decision and a fish was chosen for the pot. Inside the chosen restaurant, we were shown to a table, which had a cooking boiler at its center. They quickly prepared a wood fire beneath the boiler and the cooking process began. In went the gutted fish complete with its head and huge bulging eyes. The food in some regions of China is very hot and spicy and Harbin is one such location. I can see Jack now scooping out lots of chilies from the pot knowing that the food would otherwise be too hot for my taste.

The only wine on the menu was a locally produced brew called "Dynasty". It was awful and I only managed to sip the odd glass not wishing to offend Jack or our hosts for the evening.

The fish was also unpleasant and thankfully we were soon back in the taxi to return to our hotel. Next morning Jack was unusually late for breakfast and it was many months afterwards that he admitted he had been poorly after our Harbin fish supper. When I think back to that chemical leak, it is frightening, there had been a release into the river of benzene and surely fish of that size would have been in the river at that time. It was probably the disinfectant effects of the Dynasty wine that kept me from infection; it certainly tasted like a kind of sterilising solution and is sometimes referred to as "dysentery".

**Shopping**
The shopping in China was very good, particularly the copy market in Shanghai where I could purchase "North Face Jackets", "Prada" Handbags & "Lacoste" shirts.

**Jack Xiao in Tiananmen Square, Beijing 2005**

On one trip, my granddaughter Daisy had asked if I could bring her a pink leather handbag similar to the one I had previously bought for her mother. Not really knowing what size of bag to purchase for Daisy, I asked her to prepare a paper template to help me make the right choice.

There wasn't an opportunity to visit the market in Shanghai as Jack and I departed for Chongqing shortly after my arrival in China.

We checked into the HuangJia Grand Hotel and after freshening up, I made my way to the reception asking if they knew of any nearby shops where I might buy Daisy's handbag. Communication was very difficult and following a lot of gesticulation on my part, they called the manager. When the lady manager arrived she had further discussion with the receptionist and then said to me "I will arrange for a girl to come to your room shortly". Oh my goodness I thought, they think I am after a prostitute. "No no no" I said and pulled out of my pocket, the small paper template. There was further debate in Chinese and the manager turned to me and said, "we understand now that you are looking for a little girl and we will arrange it. Again, no no no, forget it, I waited until Jack appeared and naturally he was very amused by my experience.

Later on in the trip, I was able to make my purchase and the bag is still in good shape.


## Memories of China

As already stated, shortly before my retirement, I made my last business trip to China, accompanied by my appointed successor Francois Coeur.

Apparently, the name Francois is difficult to pronounce by Chinese speaking people and this became evident soon after our first meeting with Jack. When Jack referred to Francois is sounded more like "Francisco".

Jack soon came up with a solution and Francois became Lao Fan, which has the following meaning in Chinese; Lao means senior and experience, and Fan is a famous Chinese name, therefore, Lao Fan is a honorary name full of respect.

From China, Francois and I travelled on to South Korea where our Distributor had similar pronunciation problems to Jack. In South Korea, Francois was christened Sante.

Francois was excellent company during my last business trip and it was a pleasure to hand over to such a pleasant and capable person.

I have many memories of China and I was pleased to take Pat on a trip to Shanghai shortly after my retirement. We had a wonderful time and felt very safe, doing our own things including sightseeing and shopping.

We met up with Jack who kindly took us to Hangzhou where we visited West Lake, and what a wonderful place that is.

We also met an ex colleague of mine who took us to the city of Wuxi on the Bullet train.

My very first visit to China was in 1967; on the Blue Funnel ship "Talthybius". What I saw all those years later in 2004 was a remarkable difference. Each year since then as I have travelled all over the country, I have seen dramatic development and I foresee that in not too many years from now, China will no doubt me the largest global economy. I like the place, the friendly nature of the people and above all, their attitude to work; I really do believe that we could learn a great deal from the Chinese culture.

**Thanks to James Walker**

I am eternally grateful to James Walker for the opportunity to complete almost forty years continual employment, doing work that I enjoyed. My various roles gave me the opportunity to advance my technical and business knowledge, and to have some experience of most global industries. My work provided the opportunity for me to stand along side a Vanguard Nuclear Submarine whilst in dry dock. This is a sight to behold and when you have been close up to one of these vessels with its 16 Trident missile pod doors open, you can appreciate the firepower of this enormous vessel. I have also worked on the latest Euro Fighter and Challenger Tanks. I've met lots of very interesting people and made good friends both from the James Walker global organization as well as customer contacts along the way.

Latterly. I have been able to travel the World seeing many places that are well off the usual tourist track.

I feel privileged and honoured to have served all those years.

Thank you James Walker, it was great.

# 5

## Over forty years married to Pat

### Humble Beginnings

Pat and I were married on 5th April 1969 at St Luke's church in Leek, Staffordshire.

I remember having a few drinks with my best man and brother-in-law Cyril Edwards in the Talbot hotel before the wedding service. We must have been cutting things fine because my mother came marching into the hotel and ordered me to get into church.

Following the wedding breakfast Pat and I set off on our honeymoon, driving north on the M6 motorway with North Berwick being our final destination. It was late evening as we approached Beattock and we decided to find suitable accommodation for the night, and then continue our journey next morning. Driving into Beattock town we saw the Beattock hotel and made enquiries about rooms.

We had no problems booking in and we were given a very nice room with three beds. It was old fashioned even for those days but it was clean and tidy and fit for our purpose.

Naturally, we retired early that evening following a few drinks in the lounge bar. Next morning, when I returned to our room from the bathroom, Pat was sat on the bed shedding lots of tears. Oh my goodness I thought, something has gone badly wrong, either she has had second thoughts about her choice of husband, or I wasn't up to her expectations of our wedding night. "What's the matter", I said. "I've lost my wedding ring", she replied. We stripped the bed but there was no sign of it. "Don't worry", I said, it must be around somewhere as it was on your finger when we stood at the bar enjoying our nightcap. We searched the room with no luck and then I went to the bathroom along the corridor where she had visited in the night. There were no signs of the ring there but I did notice that the wash hand basin had a large outlet with no mesh to prevent anything falling in. I bet its gone down there I thought and immediately sent for a porter to dismantle the swan neck bend. The Porter arrived carrying a Stillson wrench and began dismantling the screwed connections. He struggled and very soon, sweat was pouring off him as the pipe joints were covered in multiple layers of paint and I guess the thing had not been apart for many years.

Eventually after much pulling and straining, the porter managed to separate the joints but alas, there was no sign of a wedding ring.

By this time I had given up on ever finding the ring and I was planning to purchase a replacement. I went down to the reception where upon I was asked if I knew anyone who had lost a wedding ring. My face must have lit up and very soon I was able to return to our room and break the news to Pat. All's well that ends well, and we continued on our honeymoon.

We had little money between us so getting started with a property was not easy. We were very lucky to obtain a rented end of terrace house at number 50 Duke Street, Leek. It was a typical two up two down with an outside loo, but we made it into a very cozy little home, adequate for the two of us. It had a large cellar where I used to make homemade wine and beer. Occasionally, I would entertain friends in the cellar, inviting them to sample the various brews on offer. Several have left late in the evening in a very sorry state, worse for wear after over indulgence.

The guy next door was a character having lived in this type of property all his life; he had no inhibitions what so ever, particularly with regard to the use of the outside toilet. I can clearly recall typically on a Sunday morning, Alf would emerge from his back door and stroll across the communal yard where usually there would be a couple of lady's engaged in polite conversation. "Good morning ladies" he would say as he made his way towards the loo. Soon after, all hell would break out, as Alf did his duty in a very noisy fashion. We were so self-conscious over the use of this convenience that we were careful not to make any sound even from the rustling of paper. Not Alf though, he would let rip as if it was the normal thing to do.

We needed to save our pennies and after a couple of years we managed to secure a mortgage and move into a new-detached property at Knypersley not too far away. Looking back, they were good days at the terraced cottage although as in most bits of my life they were not

98

without incidents, some good and some not so good. On the lighter side, I remember Pat purchasing a nice joint of beef from the butchers shop at the bottom of the hill and having placed it on the luggage tray of her new Mothercare pram, an Alsatian dog came up and nicked it, we were both very peed off about that and probably had to make do with sausages.

I can also recall a more positive incident as we were walking out with the pram one very wet Sunday afternoon. Saving very hard for our own property, money was quite scarce and I said "wouldn't it be grand if we found a fiver." No sooner said, there appeared a fiver on the pavement in from of us. What a blessing that was and having sorted a baby sitter for the evening, we had a very nice night out as you could with less than a fiver in those days.

We moved into our new property at Knypersley, which was very nice, but cash was very tight to deck it out. We managed to fit the lounge diner with carpet but we had no funds available to purchase stair carpet. I mentioned the fact to my manager Wilf Seabridge who suggested that I take home some rolls of Nebar gasket material, which had exceeded its shelf life. Nebar is a James Walker proprietary jointing manufactured from rubberised cork. It is a top of the range material and certainly not intended to be used as stair treads. However, needs must and I cut the sheets into suitable size pieces, which I then glued onto the wooden stairs. They didn't look particularly pretty but at least they deadened the sound and served a purpose whilst we saved our pennies towards a proper carpet.

We had very nice neighbors and the man of the house professed to being an amateur artist. One day, we were invited in and I couldn't believe what they had hanging over the fireplace. It was one of his paintings, a portrait of the daughter and it was unbelievably poor with no frame just a painting on the reverse side of a sheet of hardboard. There was another picture on an adjacent wall; this was a rural scene showing a very blue canal with several cows in a field. As with the portrait, this had to be seen to be believed.

We were returning home one day and as I parked the car on our drive, who should appear but Fred next door pushing a wheelbarrow. He tipped out a pile of concrete that he then began to spread with a spade. "What are you doing Fred," I asked, "making a pathway around the house", he replied. "Fred," I said, "you need to place some wooden shuttering either side the path so that you can tamper the concrete down to a required level". "It will be alright" he said and continued as before, just tipping the concrete and then spreading it about with his garden spade. When it was finished his wife painted the path red and when the rains came, there were enough puddles of water for ducks to land.

On another occasion, we could hear a lot of banging and when I peered over the fence, I could see Fred hammering away at some planks of wood that he had placed on the ground. "What are you up to?" I asked, being the nosy neighbour I am. "Building a shed" Fred replied. You can imagine what the finished construction looked like as he completed the floor first and then worked upwards. By the time it was finished, it took on a geometric shape that is difficult to describe, but there were no vertical and horizontal lines, just angles. Good old Fred, I shall never forget him.

### The joys of camping

Holidays were a problem in the early days, we didn't have many, and they were difficult to afford. Camping seemed to be the solution so I went out and purchased a second hand tent with just the minimal amount of equipment to get us started. It was a used tent, the type they advertised and sold through national newspapers. It was a bit grubby so I painted the roof bright blue and the walls a striking orange, using proper materials for the job, of course.

Our very first outing was to Conway North Wales where we pitched up at the "Puffin" Camping Park. After a bit of a struggle, we got ourselves sorted and decided to take a little trip out in the car. By this time, we had Robert as well as daughter Tracey and we had purchased a little fabric sleeping cot for the baby lad. As we were driving out across Anglesey, we noticed the sky becoming very dark and we decided to turn round and head for what we thought would be the safety of our tent. By the time we reached the camp site there was a gale blowing the likes of which we had not experienced before and to my horror the tent was almost down, with the collapse of the veranda poles and the extension cover was up in the air like the sail on a ship. Following a few frantic minutes, I got matters under control and we all managed to get inside for shelter. There came a fellow camper to our tent door and asked whether I had experienced camping before. "No," I said, and he thought that would be my response. We asked why he had posed the question. He commented that I had pitched beneath a very large oak tree and with the very bad weather about to close in; we could be in danger from falling branches. I went outside and surveyed the situation and then decided to risk it.

We had one hell of a night, and I spent several sessions swinging on the tent frame in order to prevent the whole set-up from blowing away. You could hear pots and pans blowing around the site and people were shouting – it was awful. At about three in the morning, I decided to make a cup of tea but abandoned the idea when flames from the gas cooker shot two feet into the air.

Next morning the gale had calmed down and when we looked out there was almost total devastation, with nearly all the other tents on site, either in taters or collapsed under the strain of the severe storm. Our £25 second hand MFI tent had served us well and I felt quite proud of my achievement in keeping us safe even from falling timber. I was not so pleased when Pat described it as looking like something Colonel Gaddafi of Libya might live in!

Having got some experience of camping, we ventured out and bought ourselves a nice new tent with proper beds and cooking facilities. We spent some of our best holidays camping, usually visiting the same site on Farmer Johnnie's farm at Tydweiliog on the Lynn Peninsula in North Wales.

There were other incidents like the time I was loading up the roof rack preparing for another camping trip. It was raining heavily so I decided to load up with the car inside our new garage that I had recently built. This had been part of a big project that included the fitting of new wrought iron gates and the laying of a tar-macadam driveway. The garage had a very smart cedar wood up and over door of which we were very proud.

Having loaded up and looking very much as if were taking everything including the kitchen sink; I got all on board and started to reverse the car from the garage. There was such a bang and oh dear; the load on top had collided with the door causing considerable damage. I had to make things as secure as possible leaving proper repairs until our return. Feeling rather peed off, I started to reverse the car down the drive towards the newly erected wrought iron gates and as we approached the entrance, there was another very unhealthy sound, this time from underneath the car. I leapt out and to my horror, I could see that with the weight of the load, the car was low on its suspension and it had fowled on top of the angle iron gate stop that I had cemented into the driveway. Now even more peed off, I decided that rather than remove the load from the car, I would reduce the height of the metal gate stop by means of a hacksaw. We finally got on our way with many critical comments coming from the rear seat.

We acquired a pet tortoise, which we christened Henrietta and of course, Henrietta would accompany us on camping holidays to Tydweiliog. I would tether Henrietta to a tent pole by means of a piece of string and for several holidays everything worked fine.

Unfortunately on one such visit, I checked to see whether Henrietta was happy with her lot, when I discovered that she had escaped. There was just the length of string but no signs of a tortoise. I didn't dare say any thing to Pat and the kids but having looked around the immediate vicinity to no effect, I had to come clean. All hell broke out, with the children crying and Pat accusing me of gross negligence.

It was a Bank holiday and Farmer Johnnie's field was packed to capacity. You can imagine some of the looks I received as I made my way round the camp sight asking if anyone had seen a tortoise. "A what!" someone said, "you have to be joking." I searched all over the field but alas; Henrietta was nowhere to be seen. My life was miserable, with the silent treatment from Pat and looks of disgust from the kids.

A couple of days past and we had given up any possibility of ever seeing Henrietta again. I was sat outside the tent when I spotted farmer Johnnie's wife coming across the field with Henrietta clutched very firmly in both her hands. What a miracle we thought, and once again we were a complete and happy family. Apparently someone had found Henrietta in a field more than a mile away and had then made enquiries at surrounding premises. Pat insisted that from then on Henrietta would have to stay inside the tent in a large cardboard box for the remainder of our holiday. How good it was to have family life back to normal and I decided to celebrate that afternoon with a few beers.

In the evening, Farmer Johnnie paid us a visit to say how pleased he was to hear the latest news of Henrietta. He asked if he could see her and I brought her out of the tent for him to view. We stood chatting for a few minutes and then Pat said dinner would be ready very shortly. I made my excuses to Farmer Jonnie and then nipped to the ablutions block for a quick shower before we dined. All the beers had been consumed and I was still feeling very happy following the miraculous return of Henrietta. I was in the hot shower when all at once it dawned upon me. Oh my goodness I thought I've left the damn tortoise outside the tent. I hurried as fast as I could to finish my shower, I then ran back to the tent but alas Henrietta had gone.

Can you imagine my embarrassment as I went all around the campsite again asking if anyone had seen a tortoise? "Not you again" someone said and I felt like some kind of crazy man.

The family was once again distraught and I could see a divorce on the horizon. Desperate, I didn't know what to do next. Sat there with my head in my hands I just spotted something sticking out from under the tent ground flap. Thank God when I lifted the flap, there sat Henrietta. Gee that was a relief and needless to say, from then on, I took great care to watch over her, as I couldn't have coped with those stress levels ever again.


Very often I would take a five-gallon tub of home brewed beer to Tydwieliog and on one such occasion, we were travelling along and Pat commented that it was starting to rain. How could it be raining I thought out of a clear blue sky. Then it dawned on me that maybe the beer barrel on the roof of the car might be leaking. I stopped at a convenient location and upon investigation found that not only had the beer been leaking but also it had soaked all the pillows upon which I had rested it to ensure a safe journey. Once again the air was blue and for a couple of nights we all had to sleep on pillows that smelled of home brewed ale. It didn't do us any harm and I personally slept like a baby.

I have one more amusing recollection of Tydwieliog, when we arrived there were no tents whatsoever on the field. After some consideration, we decide to pitch at the top of the field facing the sea. I had just finished erecting the rig when another car pulled onto the field. It was a guy from Liverpool whom I had met on previous visits to Farmer Johnnies field. He got out of his car and came across to me and asked if I objected to him pitching alongside, providing he left a reasonable gap. I had no problem with this, as it was always nice to have another tent close by for security reasons. I knew this family and they were all very pleasant. He set to and when he had finished, like us, he left to visit the beach.

A couple hours later when we returned to the site I could not believe that someone had pitched their tent in between us leaving a gap either side of less that 12 inches. The guy from Liverpool was furious and said that the chap in the third tent would almost be sleeping in his bed.

There is a name for this and haven't you ever parked your car at the end of the supermarket car park way away from any other vehicles, only to return and find that someone has parked adjacent to you, even though there were loads of spaces elsewhere.

**Holidays abroad**

As things became a little easier financially, we decided to take at least one continental holiday a year. They were ok but I generally suffered with a bad stomach, which spoilt the majority of trips. Following several situations where I had been ill on holiday, we were away for two weeks in Cyprus and decided to take an excursion to Egypt on the MV Prinsessa Marissa. This was towards the end of the first week and we sailed overnight, spent the following day seeing the sights and then returning that night. I had been under very strict instructions about what I should not eat or drink whilst on this trip, obviously because of my past record. Pat provided wet wipes for cleansing our hands before touching anything that might be consumed.

The trip was marvellous but on the return journey I began to feel very ill. I kept thinking to myself that maybe it would pass if I kept quite about things because I knew what abuse I would face if once again I had to take to my bed. I am very rarely physically sick but I was going at the other end at a remarkable rate.

When we returned to Cyprus I was unable to conceal my discomfort and Pat prescribed some stomach tablets that her brother Roger had provided just in case I might encounter my usual problems.

Things got worse, and I became scared that I might be having some kind of heart attack. I kept going until 3.00am and then asked Pat to call a doctor. Having examined me he said that he would have to take me into hospital for some tests and upon arrival, I was met by the director doctor who shook my hand and assured me that he would help me get well very soon.

I was put into a side ward, which had two single beds and sliding doors opening into a clinic area where day surgery visitors would assemble. It was not very private but I had no choice but to get on with it. Several times during the first day the director doctor would open the sliding doors bend his arm upwards and say, "You have to be strong."

As evening approached he came back again and said that he would get me a very nice young lady for the night. They took specimens for culture tests and I was given one dose of morphine, which made me feel a lot better.

At about nine o'clock in the evening I lay in my bed feeling very poorly with the relief of the morphine long gone and again the doctor returned. This time he had a very attractive young lady with him who was scantily clad in a white tea shirt and very brief red shorts. After some examination, he settled her down into the single bed along side mine and the lights were dimmed for the night. I lay there in tortous pain wishing that I could get a little relief from the severe stomach cramps. Once I was aware that the young lady was sound asleep, I tried to achieve a little relief by parting with some wind. Being very careful not to make any noise, I finally managed to produce a little fart, which was like a blessing from heaven. What relief this provided and before too long I was doing them on a regular basis. The stench was horrendous but after all I thought, this is a hospital and these things are expected.

As morning approached, I was still passing wind and my pain was at a lower intensity.

For some reason, I put my hand down the bed and nearly fainted when I realised that it was not only wind that I had been passing and the bed was wet through with diarrhea. The mattress had no protective cover and the contents of my bowels had well and truly soaked in. I felt dreadfully embarrassed and wished I could escape from this horrible situation.

I realised that I would have to report the situation at some stage and face any consequences by way of a reprimand.

The young lady was still asleep when her boy friend came to visit. They were kissing and cuddling and I overheard him whisper to her "What's the matter with him". People began to gather in the waiting room chairs just outside our ward and I thought it was time to take some positive action. My bowels were about to explode again and I had to get myself to the toilet, which was situated out of the doors and along a corridor down to the right. My problem was that I would be in full view of those in the waiting room as I made my dash.

I spoke out to the kissing couple that I was very embarrassed about my situation and needed to visit the toilet. An added problem was my intravenous drip stand which had to go everywhere with me. I got out of bed with my pyjama bottoms very wet and stained and wheeled my drip stand along to the toilet. When I got there totally embarrassed, the door was locked and I had no alternative to make my way back to my bed. As I entered the ward, the young male visitor was laid on his back with his knees in the air and in fits of laughter. I was very annoyed and made it perfectly clear that it was all right for him but he should consider my dreadful situation.

Once I informed the nurse of my plight, I was moved to another ward where I had total privacy and things began to improve. Pat and the kids visited me twice a day and I can see them now always with an air freshener which they periodically sprayed in my direction.

I'll cut this short now as the story goes on. I had to tell lies about my toilets and intake of food before the doctor would agree to me travelling home. Back in England, I had to report to the public health department and I was diagnosed as being a salmonella carrier. Needless to say, I survived but it took a long time for me to recover to full strength.

Another bad holiday experienced occurred when Pat and I together with Tracey visited Portugal. It was a last minute booking for one week in Yugoslavia. We arrived late and after checking-in, Tracey and I decided to have a look around and find the swimming pool.

To our dismay, the hotel did not have a pool; instead there was a bathing area, which was part of the sea. There was a walled area, which maintained some depth of water and whilst we were disappointed, agreed that we should make the best of things.

Next morning, all three of us made our way to the swimming area, bathing towels were laid out and I was ready to take a paddle. "Are you putting anything on your feet" said Pat as we had flip-flops and pumps if required. I looked around and the sea was alive mainly with young kids jumping in and out a generally splashing around. "No need for foot ware" I replied and stepped into the brink. I guess I took no more that half a dozen steps when I was stricken with intense pain in my left foot. With the water only up to my knees, I was able to lift my leg out to observe what had happed. My initial reaction was that I had trod on some broken glass but this was not the case. Sticking out of my foot were lots of black spines and it was obvious that I had stepped on a spiny sea urchin. I then heard Pat say "what has he done now," as I hauled myself out of the water. Tracey yelled "hold him down Mother whilst I pull them out." Between them they did remove most of the spines but my foot was still very painful and for the remainder of the week, I hobbled about walking only on my tiptoes with my left foot.

I did have to smile on the last morning, as I was sat outside waiting for the courtesy coach to the airport; the hotel front door opened and out hobbled a middle aged man obviously in great difficulty with one of his feet. I laughed inwardly as I could guess what had happened to him.

Once at home I visited the doctor who said there would be several spines still lodged in my foot but the best course of action was to wait and in time, they would come out naturally. He was right but it was eighteen months after the event that I was able to squeeze out the final brute.

We once had a holiday almost spoilt by a little lad on the same trip. Pat and I were on board our outward-bound aircraft when an angelic little face appeared over the seat on front. I probably made a very big mistake by either winking my eye or sticking out my tongue and whichever; it brought great amusement to the little chap. For a short period we were well entertained by his cheeky face and broad smile. All was fine until the stewardess insisted that he be strapped into a harness attached to his mother's seat belt. He screamed alarmingly and it persisted until the seat belt sign was switched off. Almost immediately he was up peering over the seat once again with an affectionate smile. By now we knew that his name was Daniel because his mother was saying it at least six times a minute. "Sit down Daniel," "be still Daniel," "turn around Daniel" and so it went on.

By now we had had enough of Daniel and as the two hour fight was near its end we were looking forward to getting as far away from Daniel as possible.

I recall saying to Pat as we walked off the aircraft "thank goodness for that, peace and quite at last."

We collected our luggage and cleared customers and made our way to meet the holiday representative. She checked our hotel reservation and asked us to walk to the coach park and board bus number 16. You'll never guess who was on the same bus and already screaming as loud as ever. Fortunately we were only on the bus for a few minutes but I was extremely worried when you've guessed it, Daniel and his parents left the bus at the same hotel complex as us. Never mind I said this is a very big place with about four huge accommodation buildings.

We checked in and got to our room where it was time for a stiff drink and then, settle down for the night.

Next morning we were up and still talking about the horror of Daniel when who should be peeping under the balcony partition from the adjacent room, you've guessed it, Daniel.

This had been a cheap holiday and there was little to do and not much excitement to be had. We escaped from Daniel and retuned to our room in the afternoon. Obviously very hyperactive, Daniel needed a sleep in the afternoon and at about 3.30pm Daniel's mother would read the little lad a story in order to induce sleep. Sitting out on our balcony taking the afternoon sun, Pat and I quite enjoyed listening to the story; apart from every few seconds it was interrupted by his mother's load voice saying, "Go to sleep Daniel." Occasionally, she would burst out with "for God sake Daniel go to sleep."

For the entire week, we made our way back to our balcony in readiness for the afternoon story. They were all very good and as time went on we found Daniel's mothers frequent outbursts quite amusing.

On one occasion, We could hear Daniel's mother saying "Daniel come away from the balcony railings", this was repeated over and over again, then the little chap must have come running out of the room heading for the railings and we heard his mothers shout "good God he's gone over the balcony." I know it sounds very cruel but thank the Lord for that I thought. I didn't really wish to see him hurt and fortunately she just managed to catch hold of him before he went over the edge.

On the last evening, we met up with Daniel and his parents and I entertained them by relating our experiences of Daniel from our first encounter on the outward-bound flight. They were nice people and were not offended by my comments. We had a pleasant evening and they explained that they had had Daniel late on in their marriage and they admitted that he had been totally spoilt.

Towards the end of the evening Daniel suddenly took off at great speed heading towards the harbour wall. His father chased after him and made a desperate rugby tackle grabbing Daniel just before he was about to leap into the sea. I remember thinking; I would have let him go because he wouldn't have done it again. He totally dominated his parent's lives and I thought a good clip around the ear would soon put Daniel on the right path towards better behavior.

One final holiday incident for the record involves an accident, which could have been much worse. Pat and I were on holiday with Robert staying in a very nice apartment, which had two sets of patio doors leading to a long balcony.

We had been out for a meal plus a few drinks and upon our return to the apartment; I asked Robert to open the patio doors so that we could sit out in the evening air and partake of a nightcap.

I heard the door slide open as I was leaving the toilet and made my way towards the balcony. It was dark outside and the only light switched on in our apartment was from a bedside lamp. I hadn't realised that the door that Robert had opened was the one from the master bedroom and not the one that I was fast approaching. Bang, I walked straight into the closed glass door and bounced off it and fell to the floor. I was badly bruised in the face and winded with shock. Pat and Robert were in fits of laughter, it must have seemed funny to them but in days before the invention of safety glass, very serious injuries have occurred in similar situations.

## Cinematography

Pat's brother Roger lives in Leek and when we moved there for the second time, Roger and I would have the occasional pint at the British Legion Club.

One evening, we were propping the bar up with an old mate, Keith Drury when Keith informed us that he had acquired some blue movies but had no means of viewing them. At that time Roger was living alone at 30 Haregate Road and we decided to put on a film show to invited guests. Roger was able to borrow a 8mm projector and with the films from Keith, we set a date for the showing. Verbal invitations were given to friends who were each asked to bring along a few beers.

As neither Roger nor I had any experience of film projectors, we agreed that it would be prudent to have a trial run and for this we set aside the night before the big performance.

Through trial and error, we managed to thread the film and we were about ready to begin the rehearsal. We hadn't thought about a screen and our only option at this late stage was to project directly onto the curtains.

The lights were dimmed and I switched on the projector and the show began. We sat there enthralled and were excited that this would be a great success the following night. I don't know how much film there was on each reel but as I recall they were about 12 inches in diameter and I think they provided about thirty minutes viewing.

As the first show was coming to an end, I became aware of something floating around me as I sat on a chair behind the projector. When I investigated it became apparent that the film had not been winding onto the empty reel and it had all built up in an enormous heap around me. Roger switched the light on and we couldn't believe our eyes, it was a hell of a mess and there was nothing for it but to sit for hours slowly untangling the film and winding it back on to the original reel.

Come the day of the performance and once all the guests had arrived and beers were served, we started the show and it was a great success. Some of the comments were classic and far too rude for this publication but about half way through, there came a loud knock at the door and I immediately feared that some neighbour had seen the projection on the lounge curtains and we had been reported to the police. Fortunately, it was someone who wished to speak to Roger and all the guests sat in absolute silence whilst the matter was dealt with at the front door.

To this day, I dread to think what might have happened and how naive we were to project such material onto the curtains. It might be the case that some old widow, might well have enjoyed the film but I cannot get it clear in my mind whether everything would be in reverse on the other side of the curtain!!

### Vicar and a Tart

It was a relative's wedding and Roger persuaded me to go to the evening do in fancy dress. He had the idea that he would go as a vicar if I would dress as a tart.

We turned up at the do with Roger looking just like the real thing complete with dog collar and reading spectacles. I was wearing a brightly coloured dress that was very distinctive and selected on the basis that no one else could possibly be wearing the same.

I was very sexy with black stockings and suspenders and of course this very distinctive dress.

Needless so say, we amused those present all except one lady who was wearing the exact same dress as me. Poor lady she must have felt extremely embarrassed. Almost as much as me when I had to pay a penny and you can guess how surprised the men in the urinal were when I lifted my skirt to have a pee.


## A bad day out in Blackpool

Times were tough when our children were very young and I clearly recall a day out in Blackpool that really peed me off.

Our first child Tracey was still a baby and whilst very beautiful, she suffered from projectile vomiting, very often straight after her bottle-feed. Whilst I can count on one hand the number of occasions when I have been physically sick, I do have a very tickled stomach and the least smell of vomit or the briefest glimpse of some wrenching, makes me automatically heave out of control.

On the day in question, Pat and I had decided to take Tracey to Blackpool where Mother and Father in law (Joan and Jack) were staying on holiday. Pat gave Tracey her morning feed and everything seemed ok with no signs of the feed coming back. We loaded the car with all the things required to support a babe in arms and off we set. We were nicely heading north on the M6 motorway when I was hit in the neck by a fountain of warm milky vomit fired from behind where Tracey was sat on her mother's knee. My reaction was no surprise what so ever and I began wrenching to a point where it was very difficult to maintain concentration on my driving. I opened the side window to grasp at some fresh air but the remainder of the journey was blighted by repeated attacks from my crippled stomach.

Upon arrival in Blackpool where it was blowing a gale and piddling down with rain, we located the guest house where Ma and Pa were staying and we cleaned up the mess as best we could, although there was no chance that we could completely get rid of the awful smell. The girls expressed a wish to go shopping so we boys decided to take a walk to the boating pool where Jack suggested we might get some shelter from the terrible weather. He was right because the pool was like an amphitheatre with high surrounding walls, which provided good protection from the wind and rain. We got ourselves a couple of deck chairs and sat there relaxing and watching the paddleboats and canoes going merrily by. After a few minutes Jack said, "Shall we take a ride in a boat." It seemed like a good idea to me so we made our way to the jetty and paid our fares for the hire of a canoe.

The boat attendant had a canoe secured to the end of a long pole with which he was keeping it in place alongside the wooden jetty. "Get in the front," said Jack and very carefully, I lowered myself into the front end of this steel boat, which seemed much heavier that I would have imagined. Having got myself into position with the rowing paddle firmly in hand I was aware of the canoe moving as Jack positioned himself into the rear of the boat. "We're off" he shouted, which I understood to mean that we were moving off. Not one bit of it, following a couple of violent wobbles the canoe capsized and we sank to the bottom. What a hell of a shock, and whilst the water was not very deep I was completely under the surface and might easily have drowned. It was a struggle getting my legs out of the damn thing and panic was about to set in when I got myself free and was able to stand up and get my head above water. As I looked round Jack stood up spitting out the dirty water and shouted out "good God, I think I've swallowed a herring".

The boat attendant was not pleased and was more concerned about how he could recover his canoe from the bottom rather than our state of health or well being. I accused the attendant of negligence and said that he should not have cast us off until it was obvious that we were stable and in a safe state to paddle our canoe. He said that Jack was to blame because rather than sitting in the bottom of the canoe he had parked his backside on the rear cover section, which raised the center of gravity and made the boat unstable.

Sat around the pool were lots of people in their deck chairs, many in fits of laughter at what they had seen. One rather plump gentleman was rocking to and fro to a point where he seemed fit to burst.

I demanded a refund from the attendant but he flatly refused. Instead he offered us another ride, which we reluctantly accepted. By this time we were feeling the effects of the cold and one lap of the pool was sufficient, so we cut the ride short. As we disembarked, a mighty roar sounded as people cheered and laughed at our misfortune. The very large man was still rocking in his chair when the canvas ripped and he fell back with his legs up in the air and flat on his back. "It's our turn to laugh Now" I said and told him it had served him right.

What could we do now? We were wringing wet through, freezing cold and desperate to get into some warm dry clothing. "Let's go to he Derby baths," said Jack, as they will have drying rooms where we can get ourselves sorted. Drying rooms I thought, I don't think so but he seemed very sure so we strode out across the promenade. What a spectacle Jack looked, he was wearing a brand new Marks & Sparks pure woolen cardigan and the weight of the water had stretched it to a point where the hem was almost down to his ankles. We got some funny looks as we waited in the queue to book the drying rooms. When it became our turn, "Drying rooms" the attendant said, no such things here we only have swimming facilities. That was enough for me, back to the boarding house where upon our arrival, the girls were returning from their shopping trip. You can imagine their amusement when we explained what had happened.

"Get in the car quick" I said, and off we set for home. By the time we arrived home in the Potteries, my clothes were almost dry but I had great difficulty removing my jeans. When they did come off, my legs were coloured blue from the dye in the cloth. What a day that had been, one, which I would like to forget.

## Sea Breezes

One of the funniest things I have ever seen occurred whilst Pat and I were onboard a cross channel ferry. We were taking a day trip to France and once away from Dover, we decided to take a walk on the deck and enjoy the sea breeze. It was a lovely summer's day with not a cloud in the sky and everything in the world seemed rosy.

We were strolling along the deck when out of the corner of one eye; I spotted a sight that every young man can only dream about. You know those box-like containers found on the deck of any typical ferry; they are used to accommodate life jackets. We were passing one such container where there were two young ladies sitting on the top with their knees up in the air. One of these ladies was wearing a pair of baggy fitting shorts and whether she had forgot or not, but she was not wearing any panties and there for all to see was her Jack & Danny. As we sauntered past, Pat spotted me looking very gingerly at the unbelievable sight and she muttered "don't look again, that is just disgusting."

As we moved on, I found somewhere for us to sit down and as we looked back towards the ladies on the life jacket container, we could observe other passers by and it was so amusing, particularly when a male got first sight of the show. I distinctly remember seeing two young guys strolling past and one caught sight and immediately began speaking out of the corner of his mouth to inform his mate of what could be seen if he glanced to the left. They passed by and then after taking a few minutes to recover from uncontrollably laughter, they would walk back for another good look.

Husbands and wives were interesting to observe as it was always the male who spotted the sight and as soon as his misses got wise, she immediately instructed her partner not to look again. It was one of those occasions when I wished I'd been wearing those reflective sunglasses where you can face forward and safely have a good stare out of the corners of your eyes.

## Jeff Banks Quality
We had been invited to a Christening and I was considering what I should wear for the occasion.

In those days, I used to purchase my business suites from a factory shop in Goole and whilst there, I spotted something very interesting on the bargain rail. It was a Jeff Banks designer suit originally priced up at £400 and on the ticket there were a number of price reductions, with a final offer price of £15. It was just my size 42 reg. and it was a light grey colour, just what I required for the forthcoming christening. I couldn't believe the price and having given it a thorough inspection, I made a purchase.

I couldn't wait to get home and show Pat what I had bought and sure enough, like me, she couldn't get over the bargain price for such a high quality garment.

I tried it on and it fitted a treat, it was a good feeling to be the proud owner of such a fine suit.

Come the day of the christening, I took the suit from my wardrobe and because it was brand new there was no need for Pat to press the trousers. I wore a white shirt with a flashy yellow tie and felt very smart indeed.

We attended the service and afterwards there was an open air, alfresco style buffet where all invitees mingled together. All was going very nicely when I spotted my son Robert in hysterics of laughter whilst pointing at me. I looked all around me but there was nothing obvious to cause such amusement. Rob as we call him is not one to keep a secret and whatever he was laughing at was soon shared with others who also began to erupt in fits of laughter.

In the end I had to approach him to find out what was going on. "There's a bloody great hole in the back of your trousers", he said. I looked around and sure enough there was a tear in the material just below my right buttock. Needles to say, I felt extremely embarrassed and couldn't wait for the afternoon to pass so that I could escape and make myself presentable.

Never again would I buy anything off the bargain rail.


**New 'Undies'**

Having just made the comment about no more bargains, we were shopping in the Cooperative super store in Leicester and Pat informed me that I was in need of some new underwear. In those days, vests were the norm therefore I required vests and pants.

It had been a long time since we made such a purchase and we were both gob-smacked at the high prices. Having given the matter much consideration, I decide to buy one pair, one of each and then repeat the process over subsequent monthly shopping trips.

The vest and pants were in our shopping trolley and when we turned the next corner, there was another display of gents' underwear at considerably lower prices. I'm talking here of one-third the price of the ones in the trolley. The quality looked good and the only difference I could see was the cheap ones were made in China.

It's at times like this when you are tested, whether to support British manufacture or say 'to hell with it' and go for the cheap variety.

These were the early days of cheap imports from China and I thought I would put the original one back on the shelf and replace them with three sets of the less expensive Chinese jobbies. Everyone loves a bargain and we returned home feeling very satisfied with our purchase.

The good feeling continued until washday and when I arrived home from work I found Pat unable to speak for laughing. She couldn't compose herself to enlighten me but disappeared and returned with a pair of the latest vest and pants that had gone through the wash earlier that day. Talk about shrinking, not 5% or 10%, no, they were now the size of dolls clothing and the only thing to do was throw them in the bin.

We both learnt from that experience, that price is not always the main factor when you are seeking value for money.

I used to tell this story to my customers when they informed me that they could buy cheaper engineering products to ones I was selling. "Remember, it's the quality that matters and the price is a secondary consideration".

I used that story many times to convince the customer that my products were much better value in the long run.


**Mind your head**

When we moved to Worksop in 1982 we took with us some lounge and dining area light fittings, which we had removed from our previous home in Leicester. The dining area light was suspended from an extendable cord and was positioned over the dining room table. We were very proud of these lights and I took great care in installing them into our new home.

We decided to decorate the lounge/dining area and to make the walls more accessible; we took the dining table outside and stood it on the patio. Whilst I was papering the walls, Pat was busy tripping in and out of the French window when I heard a loud bang. Bloody hell, she had walked straight into the lovely orange glass globe. "What the hell do you think you are doing" I shouted and quickly went over to see if the thing had been damaged. Fortunately, it was still intact but I gave her really good rollicking suggesting that if future, she pays more attention to where she was walking.

A few minutes later having got my breath back I stepped outside onto the patio to have a calming smoke of my pipe. When I'd finished, I strode back into the dining area, and bloody hell, I walked straight into the light, smashing a great chunk of glass which fell to the floor. You can imagine my embarrassment and the grief I got from my better half.

## Don't swear in front of the wife

When our son Robert was about ten years old he asked if he could have a model aircraft for Christmas, one that you build from a kit, and it must have radio controls.

We visited a model shop in Doncaster, made a purchase and the man in the shop said "do not try to fly this plane without some lessons" he gave me his telephone number and asked me to give him a call when we were ready to fly.

I have always taken the bull by the horns and instead of reading about the techniques of flying model aircraft and how the radio controls are operated, I went full speed ahead and believed we knew sufficient to get us started. Having finished the building process, we were now in possession of a splendid looking model plane. I telephoned the man at the shop and he invited us to join him at a field near to Doncaster where he was a member of a model-flying club. He asked us to meet him at a certain time and he would then give us some flying instruction.

Whilst I had been building the plane, I had noticed a small rectangular shaped orange flag attached to the radio antenna. There was number 32 on the flag and I didn't know what this meant nor did I see any reason to find out.

On the day of the flying lesson, Robert and I loaded up the plane in the back of our estate car and we made our way to Doncaster. Arriving at the field, there was an aerobatic model in German wartime livery, looping the loop and completing many impressive maneuvers. We got out of the car and I opened the tailgate to access our plane. The radio controls were laid by the side of the plane and Robert flicked the activating switch to the on position. All of a sudden, this splendid model plane performing miraculous barrel rolls etc fell from the sky and smashed into the ground. It was totally wrecked and the pilot shouted "No one is on 32" and then it registered with me, what the number signified. There in front of us was a post with a large board attached and written in chalk on this board was the number 32. It obviously showed the frequency on which the plane in the air was using thereby, warning all others with the same frequency to keep their controls switched off.

In a state of shock and panic, I put our plane back into the car and said "Robert get into the car quick," "Why dad he said, we've only just arrived." "Get in the car now" I said, I'll explain to you later what this is all about. Robert looked very bemused but I guess my facial expression indicated that all was not well and once inside the car we drove away at high speed. Whether they realised it was us that caused the crash, I shall never know but for sure, I didn't contact the shop owner ever again.

Not sure what to do next, I decided to get a book on the principles of flight applicable to flying model aircraft. I thought that if I could understand the basics, we could start off on our own and get better with experience.

It is very difficult to fly model aircraft particularly the one like ours, which was a high performance, fast moving plane. It's easy enough taking off but then you have to start a turn before it gets out of radio range. As you turn and when the plane is coming back towards you, the hand controls are reversed and if you are not careful you can easily lose control. You've guessed it, that's exactly what happened on our maiden flight. I was at the controls and things went belly up with the plane crashing into a nearby field of cabbages. We scooped up all the fragmented bits and started a process of rebuilding the damn thing. I crashed it again and repeated the building process; this time building two sets of wings and fuselages.

For our third attempt at flying, Robert had persuaded me that he should have a go. Pat wished to accompany us to a nearby-disused airfield and all pre flight preparations were completed. Robert is left-handed and he seemed very awkward in his handling of the controls.

We started the engine and lined the plane up along a nice stretch of concrete runway. I went over the take off procedure again and again, making it very clear to Robert that once the plane had reached maximum speed, you just pull back very slightly on the aileron lever and up she would go.

There was great tension and anticipation as Robert pulled back the throttle and sure enough it shot off with great speed. "Pull on the aileron lever" I said but nothing happened. "Pull the aileron," I repeated but still it was on the ground and fast approaching one of those wire link sheep fences, which lay straight ahead. I desperately shouted for him to pull on the aileron lever but it was too late and the plane shot clean through the fence, smashing it into many pieces. I'm not proud of the fact but these were the early days and the first time that Pat had heard me say the "F" word but I could not prevent myself from saying to Robert ", what the "F" were you doing.

Robert was in tears, Pat was appalled at my language in front of her and our son and there was all my rebuild work lying in bits.

We decided that flying model aircraft was not for us and I put it all back together with the spare parts and then sold it for £80. I hope the buyer had better luck than we did!!!


## Watch your feet

One of our best pastimes is walking in the countryside and one particular day, we were strolling in the woods close to Worksop when I looked down and saw Pat about to step into the biggest pile of dog dirt that you have ever seen. "Watch where you're putting your feet" I shouted and caused her to swerve and just avoid stepping into this terrible mess. Some time later upon our homeward trek, I was horrified when I accidentally trod in the same monumental pile and to make matters worse, I skidded almost losing my balance. "That will teach you not to be smart arse" my good lady retorted.


## What a spectacle

On another occasion when out walking, we were visiting nearby Sherwood Forest which is one of our favorite places. It was blowing a howling gale and lashing down with rain. Providing we are wrapped up properly, we both enjoy these conditions as it gives you a sense of fulfillment having battled against the elements.

By the time we had completed the four mile walk, we were ready to return home and settle down in comport for the evening. As we sat down in the car, I could see Pat looking at me and in fits of laughter. "What's the matter"? I said. "Look in the mirror" she responded. As I looked in the mirror I could see that there was only one lens in my glasses. You know that in a lifetime there are a few occasions when you experience what I term a good belly laugh and this was one of those situations when we laughed until we had stomach ache and felt sick.

It was amazing that I had not noticed the loss of the lens as the wind and rain had been blowing in my face most of the way.

We returned the following day when the weather was much quieter and repeated the walk in a desperate search for the missing lens. Alas it was not found and some 25 years on, one of us will often say, "keep an eye out for the lens" when we are taking this wonderful walk.

## Fire and Flood
### Firstly Fire

One New Year's Eve in the 1970s, Pat and I were peacefully watching the television when Terry next door phoned inviting us to join him and his wife Ann to see in the New Year. In those days I was a pipe smoker and Pat agreed to go providing I didn't take my pipe. She was always worrying that one-day I would do some serious damage and possibly set the house on fire. Terry was also a smoker and large cigars were his favorite drag. I knew that Terry would be having a nice cigar particularly on New Year's Eve and I sneaked my pipe into my trouser pocket and Pat was none the wiser.

We all settled down and the drinks were flowing nicely when Terry said, "Have you not brought the pipe." "No he hasn't" said Pat, but I confessed that it was with me. "Light the damn thing up," said Terry and I set about filling the bowl with St Bruno, my favourite tobacco. Pat and I were sat on the very smart three-piece suite, which was very stylish, with nice deep cushions and covered in an attractive velour fabric. Having filled the pipe, I took a box of Swan Vestos from my pocket and made a strike. To my horror, when the brimstone ignited, a bit of it flew into the air and landed between my legs onto the settee cushion. I looked down and broke into a cold sweat when I saw that there was a hole where the match end had made contact.

You can imagine the fuss and Pat went ballistic. To be fair, Terry and Ann were composed about the incident and I assured them that whatever the cost, I would have the damaged repaired. I didn't get much sleep that night and next morning had earache from Pat who said it would cost £1,000 if we had to replace the entire three piece suite.

I made enquiries about the manufacturer and after some tracking down; I located a warehouse in Doncaster who stocked the same fabric from which the original suite had been made. This fabric line was now discontinued but after much searching, a very nice gentleman located a small roll end that he kindly gave to me free of charge.

I then made an appointment for a local upholsterer to attend Terry & Ann's but to my dismay, when he saw the fabric which I had obtained he said it was no good because it was a mirror image of the one covering the suite.

My searching had to begin all over again, and finally I located a small roll of fabric with the pattern having the correct orientation and following a very stressful period, the damaged cushion was re-upholstered and everyone seemed happy with the outcome.

### Secondly, the flood

Going back to the New Year's day following my dreadful accident in setting alight Terry and Ann's settee, I now refer to my other next door neighbor Jack on the opposite side to Terry and Ann.

Jack and his house-proud wife Francis were away on holiday and had left me in charge of their bungalow whilst they were spending a month sunning themselves in Spain.

In an attempt to get back in favour with Pat, I offered to take her to Doncaster to do some shopping in the sales. Before we go, I said, I'll just check that everything at Jack and Francis's is ok. I opened the front door and to my horror, all I could see was water almost up to the depth of the front door step, and it was still flooding from the ceiling.

This was an even greater disaster than the previous night's mishap at Terry and Ann's and I spent the entire day stopping the leak from a burst pipe in the loft and mopping up. I had to lift their expensive furniture onto blocks of wood and took the decision to rip up all their carpets that were of the highest quality.

I managed to contact a friend of Jack's named Colin Attach and I set him about contacting Jack and Francis to break the news. He came to see me the following day and said that he had managed to speak to Jack. He explained that he had told him there had been a slight problem in the bungalow involving a leakage of water but they were not to worry about a thing because Chris Pownall had everything under control.

From that, I said they would envisage a bucket collecting some drips of water and never imagine that all their lovely carpets were cut up and dumped in the garage.

When they returned home a week or so later, the shock made Francis quite poorly.

Fortunately, they were well insured and new carpets were soon fitted and things on that side of our house were also back to normal.

From that New Year, the term Fire & Flood took on a new meaning to me and every time I hear it used I shiver with thoughts of that dreadful night with fire at one side and floods at the other. Hope it never happens to anyone else.

## What a bang

During the time we lived in Knypersley when both Tracey and Robert were very young, occasionally on a Sunday, we would take the family to the Wirrel where we would have a picnic on the beach at Hoylake.

One such Sunday, we had prepared our picnic and set off for the seaside and as we approached the Wirrel, we came across a number of police vehicles with loud halers, announcing an escape of gas and advising everyone to extinguish cigarettes and snub out any naked flames.

I parked the car in our usual spot, on the promenade at Hoylake not far from the lifeboat station. It was time for Robert's bottle-feed and I opened the car boot where I had a small spirit lamp, which I used to warm the bottle when placed in a saucepan of boiling water. Pat was unhappy about me lighting this spirit stove in view of the police announcements that we had just heard. I had put out my cigarette and there was no obvious smell of gas, so I decided to proceed and filled the stove with methylated spirit.

It began to rain heavily and I was trying to seek some shelter from under the boot lid. As I struck the match to light the stove, there was the biggest bang that I have ever heard before or since. The shock was such that I bounced up and nearly knocked myself unconscious by hitting my head under the boot lid. In a state of panic, I ran up the promenade like sh-t off a shovel. When I eventually stopped to look round, the life boat was putting to sea and in the sky above; I could see a smoke plume which was the remains of the warning rocket signaling the launch of the lifeboat. There was I thinking that my match had probably blown up Merseyside with thousands lying dead in the streets.

Boy did I get some earache when I returned to the car. Pat could not get over me running away and leaving the family to fend for themselves. It just goes to show how you react at times like that. I had a lump on my head the size of a duck egg, which I suppose was my punishment for not showing bravery when it was required.

## Photography - Florida

One time on holiday in Florida I had a very embarrassing situation regarding the launch of a Space Shuttle. The family had been to Disney World for the day and as the courtesy coach was dropping us off at our hotel, the driver said that if we were quick we would see the Discovery Space Shuttle launch in the Eastern sky. We dashed back to our room and Pat put on the television whilst I got prepared with my camera. The first floor of the hotel had a walkway veranda on all four sides and having made my judgment as to where east was I positioned myself not far from our room, with my SLR camera ready to take a picture.

At that moment a guy appeared with some very impressive photographic equipment including a tripod stand. He asked me where was the best position to take a shot of the imminent launch. I pointed to where I believed east to be and he began setting up his elaborate equipment. Inside our room Pat was relaying the countdown and soon she was counting down from ten to zero. The launch was a success but there was no sign of the damn thing in the sky. We then heard an almighty cheer from people in the street all pointing in the opposite direction to where me and the other guy had set-up. He took one look at me in a manner that Captain Mainwaring adopts in Dads Army when he says to Pike "you stupid boy. He gathered up his gear and disappeared around the corner but by this time, the shuttle was almost out of sight. I had a good belly laugh, which I guess was worth more to me than a perfect shot of a shuttle launch that I had already witnessed on a previous trip.

## Photography in Morocco

The family was on holiday in Spain and we decided to take an excursion to Morocco. I had not long had this SLR camera and was not too sure on how it worked. We were exploring the kasbahs when I noticed that the spool was not rotating when I pulled the lever that winds the film. There was a smart looking guy in our group who had a very expensive looking camera around his neck so I asked him for clarification about whether the spool should rotate each time the film was wound on to the next frame. I handed him my camera and upon investigation, he identified that the film had not been correctly inserted into the camera. He pointed to a dark corner where there was a doorway where he could secure maximum shielding from the very bright sunlight. For some reason, he took the strap off his expensive camera from around his neck and to my horror; he dropped his camera onto the concrete ground. It landed with a sickening thud and of course, it was completely shattered. I shall never forget the look he gave me as he handed my modestly priced camera back to me with the film properly fitted. I made it my business to keep well out of his way during the remainder of the excursion.

**Shopping in Morocco**

Towards the end of our escorted trip to Morocco, we were guided to a Kasbah for the opportunity to purchase some local crafts. The shop was full of leather and copper type goods plus a large array of rugs and carpets. Pat soon decided that in her words 'it was all a load of rubbish'. It appeared that all others on the trip apart from me had made a similar decision and they were leaving the store having made not a single purchase. As I was making a similar decision, a tall man wearing a red fez beckoned me into a hidden corner where he asked if I was interested in purchasing a gun. He showed me several guns including a modern looking pistol plus a traditional Arab gun with a very ornate handle. I asked how much he wanted for the Arab pistol to which he replied £160. "Ridiculous!" I said, I didn't have that amount of cash on my possession. I said that I would be in trouble if the customs in Spain or the UK found it on my possession but he said he would give me an invoice describing it as a replica.

It really did look very smart and I could picture it hung on the wall over our fireplace. I offered him £16 for it, which was all the cash in my pocket. There followed lots of argument and Pat came to the shop entrance saying that if I didn't leave now the coach was going without me. As I was following her to the door, the man wearing the fez shouted, "ok then," "you can have the gun for £16."

He had put it into a brown paper bag with just the tip of the butt showing out of the top. I gave him the £16 and ran out of the shop and leapt onto the bus. The driver immediately drove off and Pat said, "You haven't seriously bought anything have you?"

"Wait until you see what I have purchased," I said and I produced it from the brown paper bag. To my shock and embarrassment, it was not the gun that he had shown me whilst in the shop; rather it was a tin toy worth no more than a few pennies. Clearly, I had been well cheated and I felt a fool. Pat made the most of it telling others on the coach what had happened. As you would expect, there was lots of laughter, all at my expense.

When we finally returned to our hotel in Spain, there was a large waste bin stood outside and I threw the gun in its bag into the bin with the rest of the rubbish.


## Be careful on the roof

At each of our new properties, I made it my business to fit a television aerial to the roof and Worksop was to be no exception. I purchased all the requirements from a dealer in town and began the task with great enthusiasm.

Out came the extension ladder that we have had for many years and it was put up against the front of the house. It must have been something to do with the elevation of the property but when the ladder was fully extended, the top only rested just below the gutter on the wooden bargeboard. This had not happened with other properties when the top of the ladder extended above the rim of the roof tiles. Not seeing this as a problem, I climbed the ladder and placed all the bits and pieces onto the roof tiles and then stepped onto the roof myself. I made my way up to the chimney, where upon, I ledged myself behind the chimney wall, in a safe and comfortable position.

The first job was to secure the aerial mast that was held in position by a couple of steel frames, secured in place by steel wire lashings. That went fine and I then fitted the aerial itself and connected up the coaxial cable.

It was a lovely Saturday afternoon and I remember working up there, taking the occasional pause to admire the surrounding view. Pat was indoors working hard to prepare our new abode for habitation and all was well on the roof until I glanced down to where the ladder was located. Due to the ladder sitting below the gutter, it was not visible from where I was sitting and I was overcome by a panic attack. If you have never experienced such a thing, it's no laughing matter and I was very frightened.

For whatever reason, I have always called Pat–Fred and it was "Fred help", that I shouted down the chimney. She didn't hear me at first and I had to scream out loud "Fred" before I got her attention. She appeared below on the lawn and said, "Whatever is the matter." I explained that I had lost my bottle and she should call the fire brigade to get me down. At first she stood there in fits of laughter but then she could see that I was shaking from head to toe and realized that I was in serious trouble." Get the fire brigade," I repeated and at that moment, a white van appeared around the corner coming down the cul-de-sac and heading for our house. The van had a large ladder on its roof and Pat asked the driver if he could assist in getting me down. The driver was a nice bloke and he came to the top of my ladder and put forward a plan for my rescue.

He insisted that I would be well advised to come down the roof tiles on my feet, backwards because if I descended forwards, I could trip and he would not be able to catch me.

The plan worked but it was a dreadful experience and one that I shall never forget.

## Memories of that ladder

Thinking about that ladder reminds me of our time in Leicester when we resided at Hungarton Drive, Syston. Our next-door neighbours were a young couple and the wife was a very attractive lady. She usually wore black stockings and high heel shoes and it was always a pleasure to see her.

In those days, I used to clean our windows myself and one day when up the ladder, I looked next door and couldn't believe my eyes. There hanging on the washing line was a black and red Basque complete with suspenders.

The next time I cleaned the windows, I naturally glanced over the fence and lo and behold, there was that Basque again. From then on, our windows were never cleaner until one day, I confessed to Pat what I had seen on next door's washing line. "You fool" she said, "It's a peg bag!!!"

*It's been a pleasure sharing these memories and I trust that you have managed a smile or two. If you have enjoyed the read, please tell your friends, ask them to buy the book, and that will make me smile!!!*

Lightning Source UK Ltd.
Milton Keynes UK
10 January 2011

165434UK00001BB/140/P